Messiah's Coming
TEMPLE

*Ezekiel's Prophetic Vision
of the Future Temple*

Messiah's Coming TEMPLE

Ezekiel's Prophetic Vision of the Future Temple

JOHN W. SCHMITT & J. CARL LANEY

kregel
PUBLICATIONS

Grand Rapids, MI 49501

Messiah's Coming Temple: Ezekiel's Prophetic Vision of the Future Temple

Copyright © 1997 by John W. Schmitt

Published by Kregel Publications, a division of Kregel, Inc., P.O. Box 2607, Grand Rapids, MI 49501. Kregel Publications provides trusted, biblical publications for Christian growth and service. Your comments and suggestions are valued.

For more information about Kregel Publications, visit our web site at http://www.kregel.com.

Cover design: PAZ Design Group
Book design: Nicholas G. Richardson

Library of Congress Cataloging-in-Publication Data
Schmitt, John (John W.)
   Messiah's coming Temple: Ezekiel's prophetic vision of the future Temple / John Schmitt, J. Carl Laney.
     p.   cm.
   Includes bibliographical references.
   1. Bible—O.T. Ezekiel—Prophecies—Temple of God.
2. Temple of God—Biblical teaching. I. Laney, J. Carl.
II. Title.
BS1545.5.S36   1997   224'.4015—dc21   96-52012
                                                          CIP

ISBN 0-8254-3727-x

Printed in the United States of America

3 / 03 02 01 00 99 98

To Mrs. Helen J. Schmitt
(John's mother)
and
Dr. Stanley A. Ellisen
(Carl and John's professor)

Without the influence and timely
input of these two, the events
leading to the writing of this book
would never have occurred.

Contents

Illustrations

Foreword

Let them make me a sanctuary . . ." (Exod. 25:8). This command made possible God's promise to restore Himself to His people. Since Eden, humanity had wandered the world apart from the divine presence. Then at Mount Sinai, God returned His presence and reestablished the long lost relationship of a Creator-King to His subjects. The building of a sanctuary as a place for His holy presence would enshrine His purpose to make His people a kingdom of priests. The sin of Eden, however, remained, and the people of promise rejected the rule of their true King. So again God withdrew His presence, its symbol—the sanctuary—was destroyed, and His priestly people were exiled. Still the command remained: "Let them make me a sanctuary."

Once more, as at Sinai, God's hand reached down into the midst of exile and moved the heart of a captor-king to allow His people to follow His will (2 Chron. 36:23). The sanctuary was rebuilt and its priests restored. Yet the people remained unchanged, and the divine presence remained absent. History was about to repeat itself, but with one great difference: before the destruction, God came in the person of Messiah to make possible a change in His people and the restoration of His presence. The ultimate restoration, however, would await God's program with the church and His preparation of Israel in the Tribulation. Then God Himself would fulfill His own command, placing His Spirit within human hearts and Messiah's sanctuary in their midst (Ezek. 37:26–28). The divine presence would return (Ezek. 43:1–7), and a new kingdom of priests would minister to a world in worship (Ezek. 40–48).

This great drama of God's relationship with His people, symbolized by the Jewish Temple, is admirably portrayed by John W. Schmitt and J. Carl Laney. They have carefully surveyed the growing Temple Movement in Israel whose goal is to see a rebuilt Temple on the Temple Mount in Jerusalem. Their analysis of what the Jewish leaders who direct this movement are doing is both fresh and factual. Each author has contributed from his own area of expertise and scholarship.

John Schmitt, Executive Director of Messianic Temple Ministries, is perhaps the leading expert in the Christian world on the subject of the Messianic Temple of Ezekiel. His thorough research and detailed model of this future Temple are the painstaking product of many years of research and thought and have been recognized and well-received by Jewish leaders in Israel. Dr. J. Carl Laney, a veteran seminary professor and popular author, has extensive firsthand knowledge of Israel and the Middle East. He brings to this book not only the fruit of mature biblical scholarship but also his personal experience in dealing with these complex issues. Together they address the most crucial questions Christians ask concerning the future Temple, presenting in a readable fashion the Temple's biblical importance and prophetic significance.

While other books in recent years have presented many details concerning the coming Temple, none have focused in such an in-depth manner on the final Temple of the Millennial Age. In addition, most evangelical commentaries on Ezekiel give only limited attention to this Temple, although it is the subject of nine chapters in the book. The reasons for such a minimal treatment are usually the controversial and complex nature of the subject. Authors Schmitt and Laney are to be highly commended for correcting this deficiency and supplying this much needed information.

Today, as never before in the past two thousand years of history, both Christian and Jew are able to see active preparations in Israel that set the stage for the prophetic plan concerning the Temple. The Messianic Temple, at the junction between the end of a time of tribulation and the beginning of an age of redemption, forms the pinnacle of such aspirations. May all who long for the days of the Messiah and the culmination of God's great purpose through Him on earth be stimulated to greater expectation through this book!

J. RANDALL PRICE, President
World of the Bible Ministries, Inc.

Preface

Since its founding in 1986, I have been privileged to sit on the board of Messianic Temple Ministries, an organization founded by John W. Schmitt to research and communicate the message of Ezekiel's vision of Messiah's future Temple. Having known John from our student days at Western Seminary, I was delighted to give my support to this significant work. Over the past decade, we have seen evidence of God's blessing on Messianic Temple Ministries. John has had the opportunity to speak about the Temple in churches and Bible conferences locally as well as nationally. His model of Ezekiel's Temple has been featured on television broadcasts. The response to these presentations have been both positive and encouraging. But this is just the tip of the iceberg.

Through many providential circumstances, John has been able to meet and interact with the rabbis and leaders in Israel who are in the planning stages of building the Third Temple. They have recognized and appreciated the careful research John has done on Ezekiel's vision of the coming Temple. In fact, at this very time John is leaving for Israel to meet with the leaders of the Temple Institute. I know of no other Christian in the world who has this kind of rapport among these key leaders. And they count John as their friend.

It was in light of such exciting developments that the board of Messianic Temple Ministries began discussing how we could advance the cause of the Temple through publications. After much discussion and prayer, John and I met in my office to begin coauthoring a book on Messiah's Temple. We formulated an outline and started writing. For two years we met regularly to work on this project. We truly wrote the book together. We labored over each chapter, studying the issues and composing the text.

I am grateful for John's vision to present to the world what the Bible has revealed about Messiah's coming Temple.

God is doing some very exciting things among His people in the land of Israel! We pray that this book might have some part in preparing the way for Messiah's coming Temple.

J. CARL LANEY
Western Seminary

Acknowledgments

We would like to acknowledge the work of Mr. Ken Burkhart for the many hours he spent photographing the model and Mr. Fritz Van Tagen for the use of his Northern Light Studio.

We have a very deep appreciation for the leaders of Israel's Temple movement for their openness and friendship with John. We especially wish to thank Rabbi Yisrael Ariel, Rabbi Chiam Richman, Torah scholar Yoel Lerner, and the leaders of the Temple Mount Faithful—Gershon Salomon and Zeev Bar Tove. These men, though not endorsing every part of this book, have given consent to allow the use of their photographs. We realize the trust bestowed by this gesture and are very grateful.

We are especially appreciative to Laury Schmitt, John's wife, for her helpful suggestions regarding English grammar and style.

We are both appreciative of Dennis R. Hillman at Kregel Publications for his support of this project.

Introduction

A Temple Mount
Without a Temple

Carl:

It was twilight in Jerusalem. I was standing in the Old City where I had a splendid view of the Western Wall Plaza. The encroaching darkness produced a mysterious scene of light and shadow before me. The rays of the setting sun still glistened on the golden Dome of the Rock where the magnificent Jewish Temple once stood.

On the plaza before me shadowy figures moved about in the near darkness. Thousands of Jews slowly walked toward the Western Wall. Two thousand years ago, the ancestors of these Jewish people were streaming through the Temple gates for prayer and worship. But not this night. These Jews were coming to but a remnant of the Temple—to *HaKotel,* "the Wall." They were coming in recognition of Tisha b'Av.

Tisha b'Av—the ninth of Av [July/August] on the Jewish calendar—is a day of mourning recognized by Jewish people around the world. Many Jews fast for twenty-four hours and spend much of the day reciting the book of Lamentations and bewailing the calamities that have come upon them on the ninth of Av.

It was on this day in the year 586 B.C. that the Babylonians burned the Jewish Temple that had been built and dedicated by King Solomon. And it was on this same day in A.D. 70 that the Roman army, under Titus, destroyed the Second Temple, which was built by the Jews returning from Babylon and later beautified by King Herod.

And so the Jews gathered this night to begin their time of mourning near the site of the ancient Temple at *HaKotel,* the Wall, the Western Wall, Jerusalem's Wailing Wall. Some were dressed in simple, modest attire. Others—the ultra Orthodox—were dressed in black suits and black hats such as their ancestors in eastern Europe wore hundreds of years ago.

Many wore beards and side curls. Some were draped in their prayer shawls. Most were wearing sneakers or tennis shoes instead of their traditional black shoes, for Tisha b'Av is a day when Jews put aside such traditional comforts as leather shoes.

Lamenting the Loss of a Temple

A half moon shone brightly overhead. It illuminated the Western Wall Plaza and the golden Dome of the Rock just beyond the Wall. I watched as Jewish men stood facing the Wall to pray, rocking and swaying as an expression of their intensity. All along the Wall I saw black hats, black beards, and bobbing side curls. Little boys stood with their fathers, learning the sober tradition of lamenting. Every so often I heard a loud and united wail ascend from those at prayer.

Separating the men from the women was a six-foot screen. The women were weeping and praying as intensely as the men. Many were sitting on mats in little groups. Small children sat nearby holding dolls and small playthings.

But in spite of the peaceful prayers, there was tension in the air at the Western Wall. I counted twenty-five police and army vehicles as well as an ambulance waiting to respond. Soldiers, with weapons ready, were standing at the plaza entrances and on nearby buildings. Why was there such tension in the air? Because praying at the Wall is not quite the same as praying on the Temple Mount—the holiest place for Jewish people, where the First and Second Temples stood, where the Holy of Holies was located.

At the Wall but Not on the Mount

In ancient times, the Jewish people prayed on the Temple Mount. But there is no Temple on the mount today, and the Muslims have built two mosques where the Jewish Temple once stood. The Dome of the Rock and the Mosque of el-Aksa are regarded as among the most sacred in Islam. Their location in Jerusalem is no mere coincidence. It is the tangible expression of Muslim conviction that Islam has superseded the Jewish religion and has the right to inherit Jewish holy places.

Many devout Jews will not set foot on the Temple Mount. They fear that going up to the mount may result in their stepping on the ground that covers the ruins of the Holy of Holies. But a growing number believe that they have a right to pray on the mount where the Temple once stood, especially on Tisha b'Av.

Among this growing number are Gerson Salomon and his followers, the Temple Mount Faithful. For years, these Jewish worshipers have been visiting the Temple Mount on Tisha b'Av for prayer and meditation. But fearing that their actions might promote hostilities between Jews and Arabs, the Jerusalem police denied them permission to worship there this year.

Muslim leaders are keenly aware of the centrality of the Temple Mount in Judaism. They fear that the Jewish worshipers want to destroy the mosques and rebuild the Jewish Temple. In October of 1990, during the Feast of Tabernacles, a group of the Temple Mount Faithful attempted to ascend the Temple Mount. Even though the Jewish worshipers were turned away by police, this event triggered a stoning by the Muslims and subsequent bloodshed.

On this Tisha b'Av, Gershon Salomon, cloaked in a gunny sack as an expression of mourning, brought his Temple Mount Faithful to the very entrance of the Temple Mount. Several of them carried black flags as a sign of mourning. An aged and bearded rabbi, also wearing a gunny sack, stood among his students, shouting a rebuke at Gershon and his followers. He sought to persuade them that they risked desecrating the Most Holy Place by going up to the Temple Mount.

Although Israel's High Court ruled to grant permission for a small gathering there, the police have prohibited the Temple Mount Faithful from entering the Temple Mount. It is believed that their presence there would constitute a threat to security. Gershon and his followers were only allowed to approach the gate of the Temple Mount for a brief time of prayer.

"We shall never give up," said Salomon, "not on the Temple Mount, not on Jerusalem, not on the land of Israel. I want to say to all the world that the struggle of the Temple Mount and Eretz Israel Faithful movement is a struggle of all the Jewish and Israeli people for this holy mountain, for this city Jerusalem, the capital of Israel, and for the land of Israel. The struggle will continue and grow stronger."[1]

The Centrality of the Temple

Tisha b'Av traditions observed by Jewish people illustrate the centrality of the Jerusalem Temple in Judaism. And these activities, we believe, point to the prophetic hope of rebuilding Jerusalem's Temple. For more than two thousand years the Jewish people have lamented the destruction of their Temple. Yet there are Jews today in Israel who would like to stop mourning and start building.

Many Jews, like Gershon Salomon, would like to see the Temple rebuilt. Some are even now preparing for the rebuilding. Temple vessels are being carefully constructed. Priests are being trained. Harps, the ancient instrument of the Temple, are being manufactured in Jerusalem. As Shoshanna Harrari, the wife of a Jerusalem harp builder, said, "By the time that the Temple is ready and somebody calls out for a harp, we will be ready to supply them. That, we feel, is our destiny."[2]

In this book, we would like to share with you the amazing story of Israel's Temples—those of antiquity and those of the future. Our study will lead us into Israel's past as well as Israel's prophecies. Our goal is not simply to inform you about the exciting events ahead for God's people, Israel, because the study of God's Word should result not only in information but also in transformation. And so it is our goal to help you see how an understanding of Israel's Temples can impact your spiritual life. If you are willing to let the Spirit of God work in your heart, your reading of this book can make a difference in your life.

Why Is the Temple Important?

Some people have asked why a Christian should be interested in a Jewish Temple. Since we are under the new covenant and the Temple was under the old covenant, should the Temple really be of interest to us? And even if it is of interest, is it important enough to devote a whole book to the subject?

Circumstances surrounding contemporary society often make it difficult for us to decide what is really important. During the energy crunch of the 1970s, getting a full tank of gas was very important. Nowadays, most Americans do not give much thought to driving to a gas station and filling the tank. For my (Carl's) sixteen-year-old daughter, the most important thing in the world was getting her driver's license. But how important is that to someone turning fifty? Getting ahead in a career seems awfully important until one's youngest child leaves for college and one thinks, *I wish I had spent less time at the office and more with my kids!*

Time has a way of giving us perspective on what is really important. Most Christians would agree that the things that are material and physical have little lasting importance. Those things that are spiritually significant, however, have intrinsic value that never diminishes.

The message of the Temple has such lasting value. Its message did not die two thousand years ago when the Temple was destroyed. The message continues to be proclaimed through believers today. The Bible tells us that those who name the name of Jesus are the bearers of the Temple message. The apostle Paul states in 1 Corinthians 3:16, "Do you not know that you are a temple of God, and that the spirit of God dwells in you?" But even this is not the end of the story. God's Word proclaims that there is a future Temple that is destined to grace the earth.

Someday—and no one knows when—we shall wake up to the news that the Dome of the Rock no longer stands on the Temple Mount. God's Word predicts that another Temple is coming. This future Temple will be grander than Solomon's Temple or Herod's Temple and will become more significant than any previous Temple. This Temple will be the future center for world government.

Jesus, the Messiah, will return to this earth. He will set His feet down on the Mount of Olives and proceed across the Kidron Valley to enter His Temple on a white horse through Jerusalem's open eastern gate. When He comes to claim His kingdom, Jesus will bring with Him the saints of all the ages to share in His sovereign rule over this earth.

John:

To me, the most exciting part is that, as a child of the King through new birth in Jesus, I will have a part in Messiah's kingdom rule over this world. Jesus told His disciples that they would "sit upon twelve thrones, judging the twelve tribes of Israel" (Matt. 19:28). And the apostle Paul said, "We shall reign with Him" (2 Tim. 2:12). All who have been personally redeemed through faith in Christ will enjoy positions of authority in His future kingdom.

This Temple of the Messiah has a great deal to do with your future. Since Jerusalem will be the center of world government in the kingdom and the Temple will be the place of Messiah's throne, we may be looking at a building complex that will be our future ministry site. At least, we are considering a place that we, as administrators for the King, will frequently visit on government business.

Some people have a difficult time being interested in the subject of heaven. It seems all too hazy for them to get really excited about. They cannot understand the stories about golden streets, pearly gates, and playing harps on clouds. All this just does not seem real. If this also describes you, then I have good news for you. In the book of Ezekiel God has given us a rare look into the future. We find a three-dimensional prophecy about Messiah's future Temple. It is real. It is tangible. It has measurable dimensions. It can be built. It has been built—at least in model form.

As Christians, we should be encouraged as we visualize ourselves in Messiah's future Temple on His coronation day. Jewish tradition states that when Messiah finally comes to Jerusalem to set up His kingdom, He will ascend to the roof of the Temple, raise His arms and shout with a loud voice, "Humble ones! The time of your redemption is at hand!"[3] Can you imagine what it will be like to be in Jerusalem on the day that Jesus enters the Temple to take His throne? What will it be like to stand in the Temple courts as He ascends to the roof of the Temple, raises His hands skyward, and makes His official pronouncement of the beginning of the messianic age? Imagine the excitement as hundreds of thousands of God's people begin to sing, "All hail King Jesus, all hail Emmanuel, King of kings, Lord of lords, Bright Morning Star. . . ."[4]

Over the years, I have heard conference speakers say, "If we see each other no more until Jesus comes, I'll meet you at the eastern gate." Friends, in the pages of this book you will view that famous eastern gate. You can pick your exact meeting place. My family has a place already picked out. We decided that the eastern gate was going to be pretty congested, so we chose the southeast corner. It will not be as crowded and it will be easier to see what is going on.

To some, this may seem but a daydream. We are not living in the sweet by and by but the nasty now and now. So how can this teaching about the future Temple be a help to us? Scripture teaches that what we do now will affect our future. Our present service for God will bring rewards in His kingdom. Our struggles to keep going through discouragement and difficulty will definitely be worth it when we see Jesus. Think of what it will be like to hear Him say, "Well done," as He takes us to a prominent place to serve in His kingdom. Then it will be worth it all.

Most of us have in our memories specific days of extreme anguish. May 25, 1990, is one of those days for me. That was the day I answered the phone and heard an unfamiliar voice saying, "Mr. Schmitt, your wife and daughter have just arrived at Emmanuel Hospital. They have been involved in a serious auto accident. Your wife is being prepared for surgery and has less than a 50 percent chance of survival."

As my wife and daughter were returning from the ball park where my daughter played softball, my wife's car had been struck by a drunk driver. The car was destroyed. My daughter's injuries were serious but not life-threatening—mostly cuts and abrasions on her face from flying glass. But

Laury's life was hanging in the balance. She was in a coma from a blow to the head. She had a punctured lung, a bruised heart, and many broken bones.

I hurried to the hospital, still in shock from the phone call. After a three-hour wait, I was finally permitted to enter the recovery room where Laury had been taken after the surgery. It took a couple of minutes for me to see clearly that the person lying there in the midst of all those tubes and monitors was my wife. She did not look like herself. She was so still, so silent.

In my mind I pondered our situation. *She might never come out of this,* I thought. *And even if she survives, the brain damage may leave her in a vegetative state.* Slowly my thoughts began to shift. I remembered that God is preparing for Laury a new, glorified body for heaven. And someday I will see her standing by the southeast corner of the Temple! She will have her new, glorified body and will be beautiful, without a single flaw or cruel scar to remind us of this awful day.

You can see how the Temple holds a special importance for me, and, I hope, for you too. It enables us to understand and appreciate what eternity will be like. The Temple brings a little bit of heaven into our earthly experience.

The Temple is important for God, and it is important for us. In my study of the Bible over the last twenty-five years, I have found the Temple to be one of those things that has lasting spiritual significance. Throughout this book, we will show you why a study of Messiah's Temple is important. Let us list the reasons that will be developed in this book.

First, the Temple is important because it is the dwelling place of God on earth. God dwelt among His people in the tabernacle and in Solomon's Temple (Exod. 25:8; 1 Kings 6:13). And He promises once again to dwell among His people in a Temple (Ezek. 43:7, 9).

Second, the Temple is important because of the truth that it presents about the person and work of Christ. The articles within the Temple and the Temple court present a picture of Christ as the Light of the world, the Bread of life, and the Way to God (John 6:35; 8:12; Heb. 10:20). In studying the Temple, we discover many redemptive analogies that help us understand and fully appreciate the truth of our salvation.

Third, the Temple is important because of its place in Israel's history—both past and future. So significant is the Temple in biblical history that archaeologists divide Israel's history into two sections: First-Temple and Second-Temple periods. Although the Jewish Temple was destroyed two thousand years ago, Jews today still talk of rebuilding it.

Fourth, the Temple is important because of its place in the world's future. Although most people do not realize it, Jerusalem is destined to become the future world capital (Mic. 4:1–2). And the people of the nations will stream to Jerusalem to seek the Messiah in His Temple there (Zech. 8:20–23).

Fifth, the Temple is important because it will one day replace the Dome of the Rock. There is only one place to build Israel's future Temple, and that is on the site of its former Temple. Someday—we do not know how or when—newspaper headlines around the world will announce the destruction of the Dome of the Rock. That event will prepare the way for the rebuilding of the Temple in fulfillment of biblical prophecy.

Sixth, the Temple is important because one of the greatest enemies of God, the Antichrist, recognizes the centrality of this place in the final events of history. The Antichrist will take possession of the Temple during the Tribulation (2 Thess. 2:4). This event was foretold by Christ (Matt. 24:15) and will mark the beginning of an intense period of persecution against the people of God.

Seventh, the Temple is important because Christians will worship there during Christ's reign on earth. The prophet Ezekiel describes how the Zadokite priests will lead in worship through sacrifice and offering (Ezek. 44:15–27). Christians will have the opportunity to celebrate the greatness of God as we participate in these festive occasions.

Eighth, the Temple is important because it has the potential to encourage your spiritual life and motivate you in Christian service. On many occasions, discouraged and weary Christian workers have found that a study of the Temple brings a new enthusiasm and excitement about our part in God's plan for the ages.

Ninth, the Temple is important because it is a New Testament teaching highlighted by Jesus, Paul, and the apostle John (Matt. 24:15; 2 Thess. 2:4–8; Rev. 11:1–2). This teaching is not a peripheral but a priority issue.

Tenth, the Temple is important because it helps believers understand the realities of heaven. Jesus spoke of heaven but gave us very little information about it. Heaven seems so far away and so distant from our lives on earth, but the Temple is one aspect of the future world that we can describe, measure, and even build a model of. Most people who study the Temple begin to view the future with greater confidence.

Jerusalem Post Headline

While doing our final editing for this book, our hearts were thrilled by a headline we spotted on the second page of the *Jerusalem Post*. The headline reads, "Justice Minister Favors Temple Mount Worship."[5] The article, by journalists Bill Hutman and Evelyn Gordon, reports how Justice Minister Ya'acov Ne'eman has expressed support for permitting Jewish worship at the Temple Mount and vowed that his ministry will provide legal support for such a move. Exciting things are happening in Jerusalem!

The article goes on to quote Professor Abdul Hadi Palazzi, head of the Islamic Institute of Rome, who spoke in Jerusalem at a conference entitled, "Jerusalem: City of Law and Justice." Palazzi said that Islam recognizes the right of any man, regardless of his faith, to pray on the Temple Mount. He also said, "There is no barrier in Islam to Israeli and Jewish sovereignty on the Temple Mount. We must remember that Jerusalem is holy to Judaism, just as it is to Islam." Jewish prayer has been forbidden at the Temple Mount since 1967 on the grounds that it would incite Muslims who worship there at the el-Aksa and Dome of the Rock mosques. But news reports from Israel suggest that this may soon change.

Are You Ready?

Through the chapters of this book, we are going to explore the future—your future. We believe that this study has the potential to change your life by giving you a new perspective on eternity. May God be our teacher and the Holy Spirit our guide as we plunge into some of the most challenging and exciting prophecies of the Bible.

Endnotes

1. *Ready to Rebuild,* produced and directed by James E. DeYoung (Eugene, Ore.: Harvest House, 1992), videocassette.
2. Ibid.
3. Rabbi Yisrael Ariel, *The Odyssey of the Third Temple,* translated and adapted by Chaim Richman (Jerusalem: G. Israel Publications and Productions Ltd. and the Temple Institute, 1994), 82.
4. Copyright © 1981 Glory Alleluia Music. Administered by Tempo Music Publications, Inc. All rights reserved. Used by permission.
5. Bill Hutman and Evelyn Gordon, "Justice Minister Favors Temple Mount Worship," *Jerusalem Post,* 20 July 1996, International Edition, 2.

1

The Tabernacle: Foreshadows of the Temple

The first step toward discovering the truth about Israel's future Temple is to understand the nature and function of the tabernacle. Why the tabernacle? The answer is simple. All biblical Temples follow the basic pattern set forth and established by the tabernacle. Therefore, a study of the tabernacle is foundational for any discussion of a biblical Temple.

What would it have been like to live before the age of videotapes, overhead projectors, and photographs? That is the way it was for God's people in ancient Israel. But God, being the Master Communicator, instructed Moses to set up a special building that would illustrate spiritual truth. The tabernacle, we will discover, is God's visual display of the person and work of Christ.

God Will Dwell in the Tents of Shem

Our study of the tabernacle takes us back to a promise that God made through Noah in Genesis 9:25–27. This promise is set in the context of one of the more sordid stories of the Bible—the dishonoring of Noah. After Noah left the ark, he planted a vineyard and became drunk. He lay uncovered inside his tent when Ham, his son, entered and saw his father's nakedness. Rather than covering Noah, Ham apparently took some perverse delight in what he saw and told his two brothers. Shem and Japheth refused to indulge in such perversity and covered their father, careful to avoid viewing his nakedness.

When Noah awoke he realized what Ham, his youngest son, had done to him and pronounced a judgment on his descendants, the Canaanites (Gen. 9:25).[1] Noah then pronounced a blessing on Shem and Japheth. In verse 27 he declares, "May God enlarge Japheth, and let him dwell in the tents of Shem." It is suggested by many ancient and modern commentators that the "him" should be "Him," a direct reference to God.[2] In other words, Noah was promising that God would dwell in the tents of Shem, the chief ancestor of the Semitic, or Hebrew, people.

The Realization of a Promise

Exodus 25–40 records the fulfillment of Noah's prophetic promise in a tangible way. We read how God instructed Israel to build its tabernacle, a dwelling place for God's glory. For about four hundred years—until the building of Solomon's Temple—this tabernacle served as the focal point of Israel's worship.

Names of the Tabernacle

The different names given to the tabernacle shed some light on its nature and function. It has four names.

Sanctuary (Exod. 25:8). The term *sanctuary* is derived from the word *kadosh,* denoting that which is holy, separate, or sacred.

Tabernacle (Exod. 25:9). The term *tabernacle (mishkan)* is derived from the verb *shakan,* which means "to settle down" or "dwell" and speaks of the structure as the dwelling place for God among His people.

Tent (Exod. 26:36). The tabernacle is also referred to by *'ohel,* the common word for "tent," indicating that it is a collapsible, portable dwelling.

Tent of Meeting (Exod. 29:42). The expression *tent of meeting* reflects the fact that people gathered at the entrance of the tabernacle on special festive occasions.

Purpose of the Tabernacle

There were two primary purposes of the tabernacle. Historically, the tabernacle served as a meeting place for God and His people (Exod. 25:8; 29:43–46; 40:34–37). The Israelites did not think of the Lord as a localized deity. They recognized that He was omnipresent and could not be limited to a single place. But the tabernacle provided a central place for the people of Israel to worship their God. The furniture of the tabernacle and its ministry served to instruct the Israelite people concerning the way in which they were to maintain fellowship with God.

There is another purpose for the tabernacle in addition to the historical purpose. Many parts of the tabernacle serve as a type of Christ. A type is an Old Testament illustration that has its place and purpose in biblical history but is divinely ordained to foreshadow some New Testament truth. The tabernacle and its articles of furniture serve as visual illustrations of God's redemptive work in Christ.

Preparations for the Tabernacle (Exod. 25:1–9)

Exodus 25 records the preparations that Moses made for building the tabernacle. First, God directed Moses to invite the people to give materials toward the building of the tabernacle (v. 2). The materials provided were of great beauty and value (vv. 3–7). This text suggests that God desired for the materials used in worship to be aesthetically pleasing—in keeping with the beauty of His great person.

The purpose of building the tabernacle is revealed in verse 8. The structure was to provide a dwelling place for God among His people. What a tremendous thought! Of all the places in the universe that God could pick for a dwelling, He chose a tent in the desert with His people!

Verse 9 reveals that Moses not only received verbal instructions from God but also saw a model or vision of the heavenly tabernacle that served as a pattern for the earthly structure (Exod. 25:40; Heb. 8:5). The word *pattern* refers to a form, shape, pattern, image, or model. It is used in 1 Chronicles. 28:19 of an architect's plan. This suggests that God was the first model builder and that He enabled Moses to see this model before he constructed the tabernacle.

A Walk Through the Tabernacle

We would like you to take a walk with us—a walk through the tabernacle (see fig. 1.1). We will serve as your personal guides and point out the significant features that God used to teach His people about the coming Messiah.

The Court of the Tabernacle (Exod. 27:9–19)

The tabernacle consists of a screened-in courtyard with a tent set up in the center area. The courtyard itself measures 75 feet by 150 feet, about a third larger than the average house lot. The court is surrounded by a screen or fence that is seven and one-half feet high. As we approach from the east, we notice that there is just one entrance into the courtyard. Here we encounter our first spiritual lesson from the tabernacle. As there is just one entrance to the tabernacle, so Christ is the one door—the only way of access to the Father (John 10:9; 14:6).

The Bronze Altar (Exod. 27:1–8)

Entering the courtyard of the tabernacle, the first thing we notice is the altar of sacrifice. This altar is centrally located in the court and stands four and one-half feet high and seven and one-half feet square. It is also called the bronze altar because of its appearance and the altar of burnt offering because of its use. The horns on the four corners of the altar are used to secure the sacrifices in place (Ps. 118:27). The position of the altar near the entrance of the tabernacle reminds us of our need for atonement as the basis for approaching a holy God. The altar serves as a visual lesson, anticipating the perfect sacrifice that Christ offered on the cross (Heb. 9:14).

The Bronze Laver (Exod. 30:17–21)

Passing the bronze altar, we now come to a bronze laver filled with water. The laver is situated between the altar of burnt offering and the entrance of the tabernacle itself. The priests use the basin for their ceremonial washings prior to entering the Holy Place.

The laver, an instrument of cleansing, illustrates our need for continual spiritual cleansing from the defilement of sin. As believers in Christ, we are freed from the guilt of sin. But there is still a need for daily cleansing from sin. Such cleansing is found only in Christ. The apostle John reminds us, "If we confess our sins, He is faithful and righteous to forgive our sins and to cleanse us from all unrighteousness" (1 John 1:9).

The Tabernacle Itself (Exod. 26:1–37)

From the outside, the tabernacle looks like a long, narrow structure covered with animal skins. It measures forty-five feet long, fifteen feet wide, and fifteen feet high. Four curtains serve as the roof and walls of the tabernacle. The innermost curtain, visible only from the interior, is made of fine linen. This is covered by a curtain of black goat's hair and then a curtain of ram's skin, dyed red. The outermost curtain protects the tabernacle from the harsh desert climate and is made from the skin of some marine animal, perhaps a dolphin. There is widespread disagreement whether the colors of the four curtains teach some spiritual truth. Perhaps we could simply say that the variety of colors added to the aesthetic quality of the tabernacle.

Only the priests were permitted to enter the tabernacle, but since Christians are believer-priests, we can continue our imaginary tour. Entering the tabernacle, we find that the structure is divided into two parts—the Holy Place and the Most Holy Place. The Holy Place is like a long room—thirty feet by fifteen feet. It contains various articles of furniture that are attended to daily by the priests. The Most Holy Place (or Holy of Holies), located at the west end, is actually a fifteen-foot cube and can be entered only by the high priest on Yom Kippur, the Day of Atonement.

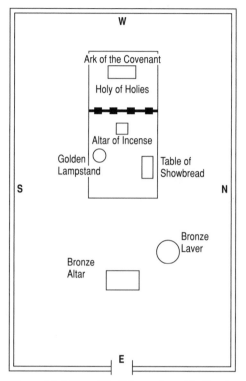

Figure 1.1 A Plan of the Tabernacle and Its Courts

The Table of Showbread (Exod. 25:23–30)

As our eyes adjust to the darkened interior of the Holy Place, we notice three articles of furniture. The first of these items—the table of showbread—stands to our right along the north side of the tabernacle. The table is made of acacia wood and is covered with gold. The rings that you notice on each corner serve as holders for the poles used to carry the table. The table holds twelve loaves of bread—one for each of the tribes of Israel. Notice also the gold plates for the twelve loaves (Lev. 24:5–9), dishes for frankincense (Lev. 24:7), and gold vessels for wine offerings.

The purpose of the table of showbread is to display the twelve loaves, which constitute a perpetual thank offering to God for His many blessings. Here we see a spiritual lesson as well. The loaves remind us of Christ who said, "I am the bread of life" (John 6:35, 48).

The Golden Lampstand (Exod. 25:31–40)

On our left, along the south side of the tabernacle, stands a beautiful, golden lampstand. It consists of an upright shaft with three branches extending from each side. The central shaft and branches are decorated with golden almonds and flowers. It is the most ornate of all the tabernacle furniture. The seven lamps burn continually with pure olive oil supplied daily by the priests (Exod. 27:20).

The lamp provides light for the priests who minister within the darkened interior of the Holy Place (Exod. 25:37). In addition, the lampstand directs our thoughts to Christ who said, "I am the light of the world" (John 8:12; 9:5).

The Altar of Incense (Exod. 30:1–10)

At the west end of the Holy Place, directly in front of the inner veil, stands the altar of incense.[3] It is also made of acacia wood and overlaid with gold. The altar of incense is considerably smaller than the bronze altar in the courtyard, measuring about one and one-half feet square and three feet high. There are four gold rings attached to the altar for the poles that are used when transporting it. The altar is used to burn incense (Exod. 30:8–9).

On the Day of Atonement, coals are taken from this altar by the high priest to burn incense in the Most Holy Place (Lev. 16:13). The smoke from the incense covers the ark of the covenant and protects the priest from the full force of God's radiant glory.

In Scripture, incense often symbolizes prayer (Ps. 141:2; Rev. 5:8; 8:3–4). As with the other articles of furniture, so does the altar of incense depict a spiritual lesson. The smoke rising from the altar reminds us of Christ's perpetual intercession for believers (Heb. 7:25).

The Veil (Exod. 26:31–35)

Before us is a lovely veil made of fine linen and ornamented with images of angelic creatures called cherubim, the plural form of the word *cherub*. The veil serves as a partition between the Holy Place and the Most Holy Place (Exod. 26:33).

According to the law, only the high priest can pass behind this veil, and then just once a year (Heb. 9:7). The veil represents the one way of access to God. The writer of Hebrews indicates that the veil represents Christ (Heb. 10:20), through whom we can approach God. The tearing of the veil at the death of Christ (Matt. 27:51) illustrates the inauguration of a new way of access into the presence of God through His sacrifice.

The Ark of the Covenant (Exod. 25:10–22)

We have reached the last stop on our imaginary tour of the tabernacle. Stepping past the veil, we have entered a fifteen-foot cubical room where the high priest was required to go once a year to make atonement for his own sins and the sins of the people of Israel. There is only one piece of furniture in this room—the ark of the covenant. The ark, about the size of a small desk (three and three-quarter feet by two and one-quarter feet), is made of acacia wood overlaid with gold. On the top of the box is the mercy seat or place of propitiation where sacrificial blood was offered. On either end of the top of the ark stand the gold images of that angelic creature, the cherub.

The ark serves as a reminder to Israel of God's personal presence in the camp. The Lord promised Moses, "I will meet with you; and from above the mercy seat, from between the two cherubim which are upon the ark of the testimony, I will speak to you" (Exod. 25:22). The ark also served as the depository of the stone tablets and later the pot of manna and Aaron's rod (Heb. 9:4). The top of the ark, commonly known as the mercy seat, is more accurately the place of propitiation. This part of the ark reminds us of the atoning work of Christ whose death served as a propitiation (satisfaction) for God's wrath (Rom. 3:25; Heb. 9:5).

The Theology of the Tabernacle

The tabernacle was erected to help the Israelites learn important lessons about God. These lessons have applications for Christians too!

The Dwelling of God

The word *tabernacle (mishkan)* means "to dwell." In Genesis 9:27 God promised to dwell in the tents of Shem. He fulfilled this promise as He dwelt in the tabernacle in the midst of the camp of Israel. This foreshadows redemptive history and reminds us that Christ came to dwell among His people (John 1:14; Rev. 21:3).

The Holiness of God

The Bible teaches us that God is holy and separated from sin (Lev. 19:2). The separation of the tabernacle altar and other furniture from the laypeople serves to illustrate this truth. Only those who were holy (literally "set apart") could approach a holy God.

The Sacrifices for Sin

Teachings regarding the tabernacle confront us with a most difficult question: "How can a holy God dwell among a sinful people?" According to God's law, this is impossible unless sin is recognized and removed through sacrifice. The tabernacle teaches us that the way of access to God is through sacrifice and the way of holiness is through separation from sin.

The Furniture

The articles of furniture in the tabernacle have great significance to us in our approach to and worship of God. The bronze altar reminds us that sin demands payment but forgiveness is available from God. The laver signifies that God demands a clean and pure life. The priest would ceremonially cleanse himself at the laver to signify the clean and pure life that God demands.

The table of showbread signifies that God is the ultimate source of spiritual sustenance for His people. Just as we cannot live in this physical world without providing food for our bodies, neither can we live spiritually without finding our food from God. The lampstand reminds us that our world is in darkness without God just as the tabernacle would be totally dark without the light of the lamp. The altar of incense represents Christ's continual ministry of intercession, and as the burning incense was a sweet savor to God, so intercession brings Him pleasure and satisfaction.

The ark, with its mercy seat, represents the presence of God Himself. He is the faithful God who keeps His promises. That is why the box is called the ark of the covenant. God has made His covenant with His people and it will not be broken. He is also a God of mercy. The mercy seat on the top of the ark represents God's mercy in relating to humanity.

As Christians we believe that all the items in the tabernacle were fulfilled in the person of Jesus Christ. Jesus became our sacrifice for sin. He gave His life as payment for our sins that had so offended God. He not only paid for our sins, but He also cleansed us from sin's defilement. Jesus gave Himself as the bread of life and the light of the world.

Later in history at the death of Christ, the veil in the Temple was torn from top to bottom; thus making both rooms one as Jesus provided a new way of access to God the Father and fulfilled the spiritual significance of the entire tabernacle.

Endnotes

1. The reason Noah cursed Canaan instead of Ham is considered by Robert B. Hughes and J. Carl Laney in *The New Bible Companion* (Wheaton: Tyndale House, 1990), 16.
2. Walter C. Kaiser, Jr., *Toward an Old Testament Theology* (Grand Rapids: Zondervan, 1978), 80–82.
3. The writer of Hebrews seems to disagree: "And behind the second veil, there was a tabernacle which is called the Holy of Holies having a golden altar of incense" (Heb. 9:4). But note that Hebrews does not say that the altar was in the Holy of Holies. Rather, the author mentions the Most Holy Place as "having an altar of incense." Although the altar stood before the veil in the Holy Place, its ritual use was connected with the Holy of Holies (see Lev. 16:12–13). The author of Hebrews was concerned with liturgical function, not physical location.

2

A Short History of Temples

John:

As I recounted in the introduction, a few years ago my wife was struck by a speeding drunken driver. As a result of her injuries, Laury was in a coma for six weeks. During those long weeks I did not know if she would recover or what handicaps she might have if she survived. Friends and family members prayed with us that God would intervene and bring Laury out of the coma. The medical prognosis was not good, but God answered our prayers. Laury has made a remarkable recovery and continues to improve.

Sometimes when life seems difficult and I feel an inclination to complain, I remember the time of that accident. I remember how bad it was during those first days, and my current problems seem to fade into insignificance by comparison. With renewed confidence, I feel ready to face any problem by God's grace.

I do not think that a person can really understand the present unless he or she is in touch with the past. We cannot appreciate the freedoms we enjoy as a nation unless we are aware of past sacrifices. So it is with Ezekiel's Temple. We cannot fully understand or appreciate the glories of Israel's future Temple unless we are acquainted with the Temples of the past. By looking to the past, we can better understand what God is doing in our day and will do in the future.

From Tabernacle to Temple

The tabernacle was erected by the Israelites at the foot of Mount Sinai in 1445 B.C., just eleven months after the Exodus from Egypt. It was central to Israel's worship and sacrificial system for about 485 years.

After the conquest of Canaan, the tabernacle was set up at Shiloh (Josh. 18:1) and remained there until about 1050 B.C. Excavations at Shiloh indicate that the city was destroyed about 1050 B.C., probably by the

Philistines (see 1 Sam. 4; Jer. 7:12). By the time of Solomon (ca. 1010 B.C.), the tabernacle and altar were situated on the high place at Gibeon (1 Chron. 21:29), possibly at the prominent hill known today as "Nebi [the prophet] Samuel." When Solomon's Temple was completed (ca. 960 B.C.), the articles of the tabernacle were taken to the Temple (1 Kings 8:4) and the earthly tabernacle then disappeared from history.

David and the Temple

When David was anointed as king of Jerusalem (ca. 1003 B.C.), he took immediate steps to bring the ark to his capitol. Amid much celebration, David brought the ark to Jerusalem and set it in a tent that had been prepared. Although this tent is not called a tabernacle, it must have functioned as such for David because he offered burnt offerings and peace offerings before the Lord there (2 Sam. 6:17–18).

After David had established himself in Jerusalem and secured his borders against invading enemies, he decided to build a Temple as a permanent resting place for the ark. But the Lord had other plans (2 Sam. 7:5). Although David was a man after God's own heart (1 Sam. 13:14), he had waged wars and had shed blood (1 Chron. 22:8, 28:3). David's son, Solomon, a man of peace, would eventually build God's house (1 Kings 6:1).

Although he was not authorized by God to build the Temple, David did acquire the site on which Solomon's Temple was later built. During a time of pestilence, David bought a threshing floor from Araunah the Jebusite and there built an altar for the Lord.

Solomon and the Temple

Although King Solomon is remembered for many things, his most significant and long-lasting accomplishment was the building of Israel's First Temple.

Why Is the Temple Important?

Reflecting on the Temple from a new-covenant perspective might lead us to question why the Temple is important at all. If God is spirit and is to be worshiped in spirit (John 4:24), why was a physical Temple necessary?

The Temple was necessary because it served to illustrate God's plan for personal redemption during a time when few people had access to God's written revelation. The Temple took over the visual function of the tabernacle. It was a place where people under the old covenant had the opportunity to develop their relationship with God through sacrifice and prayer.

Everything in the Temple serves to illustrate and remind God's people of the fact that sin separates them from a holy God. The altar points to the truth that God has provided sinners with a means of atonement. The laver reminds us of God's provision of spiritual cleansing. The incense altar reminds us of God's provision of intercessory prayer.

The Temple of God is no small matter. It is a place where people under the old covenant could meet God at His invitation. There, through sacrifice, rituals, and cleansings, they could develop their faith relationship with God.

Defining Our Terms

According to Webster's dictionary, the word *temple* refers to "an edifice for the worship of God." It is significant, however, that in the languages of the Bible (Hebrew and Greek), the term is never used specifically of a place of worship.

The basic Hebrew word for Temple is *hekal,* which means "the Temple building" (2 Kings 18:16). The term is also used of God's heavenly abode (Mic. 1:2) and means "the place where God dwells." There is a Greek word, *naos,* meaning "the sanctuary of God" (Acts 19:24), that is very similar in meaning to *hekal.* Among the heathen nations, the *naos* housed the idol of the deity being worshiped.

The Hebrew word that refers to the physical structure of the Temple, including its buildings and grounds, is *bayith.* The word is frequently used in the Bible to refer to a house and is used in 1 Kings 6:5 of the Jerusalem Temple. The Greek word corresponding to *bayith* is *hieron*, denoting a "sacred place." The word is used in the New Testament to refer to the entire Temple complex as distinct from the *naos,* the inner sanctuary.

It seems clear from these words that the biblical concept of the Temple is not just that it is a place to worship, but a dwelling—a place for God to live. Yet, the Temple is also not just a house. It is the place where God's presence is presented to His people. The Temple is God's abode, and He has given His people permission to visit Him there.

Description of Solomon's Temple

Solomon began to build the Temple in Jerusalem during the fourth year of his reign, 966 B.C. (1 Kings 6:1). First Kings 5 records how Solomon renewed an agreement with Hiram, king of Tyre, that had been first established by his father David. Solomon immediately began negotiations with Hiram to provide cedars from Lebanon for building the Temple. Hiram was happy to trade Phoenician building materials and technology for Israel's surplus wheat and oil. In addition to cedars from Lebanon, Hiram provided skilled laborers to help prepare the timbers and stones for the Temple.

The Temple that was built by Solomon was about twice the size of the tabernacle. It measured ninety feet long, thirty feet wide, and forty-five feet high (1 Kings 6:2).[1] First Kings 6:7 indicates that the Temple was prefabricated in order to minimize construction sounds and maintain a sense of reverence at the building site. The stones were prepared at the quarry and then precisely fitted together without mortar. Floors, beams, and ivory inlays were installed with wooden pegs.

There were three parts to the Temple building—the porch, the Holy Place, and the Most Holy Place. The porch, or entrance, to the Temple featured two magnificent bronze pillars standing twenty-seven feet in height (1 Kings 7:15–22). In the Holy Place were ten golden lampstands, the table of showbread, and the golden altar of incense (1 Kings 7:48–49). Separating the Holy Place from the inner sanctuary (Holy of Holies) were two doors of olive wood that featured carvings of cherubim, palm trees, and flowers.[2] Within the Most Holy Place was the ark of the covenant and two cherubim, overlaid with gold that stood fifteen feet high. The wings of the two cherubim were spread out so that they touched each other and their respective walls.

The Dedication of the Temple

Solomon took seven years to build the Temple, finishing the project in his eleventh year, 959 B.C.[3] The completion of the project was celebrated with a glorious dedication. In preparation for the dedication, the ark of the covenant was brought up from the city of David to the Temple (1 Kings 8:1). After the priests placed the ark in the Most Holy Place under the wings of the cherubim, the Shekinah glory filled the Temple, just as it had filled the tabernacle after it was erected at Mount Sinai (Exod. 40:35; 1 Kings 8:10–11). Then the people gathered at Jerusalem and observed two great feasts, the Feast of Dedication, followed by the Feast of Tabernacles—fourteen days of celebration.

It must have been at the peak of the celebration that Solomon knelt before the great altar in the court of the Temple and lifted up his hands toward heaven in prayer (1 Kings 8:54). The central feature of this great prayer is Solomon's request that God might forgive the people for future failings and restore them when they turned to Him in repentance. God's answer to Solomon's prayer is capsulized in 2 Chronicles 7:14, "And [if] My people who are called by My name humble themselves and pray, and seek My face and turn from their wicked ways, then I will hear from heaven, will forgive their sin, and will heal their land."

But the Lord goes on to say that if the people refuse to turn from their sin in repentance, then dire consequences will follow: "But if you turn away and forsake My statutes and My commandments which I have set before you and shall go and serve other gods and worship them, then I will uproot you from My land which I have given you, and this house which I have consecrated for My name I will cast out of My sight, and I will make it a proverb and a byword among all peoples" (2 Chron. 7:19–20).

This divine warning is a key to much of Israel's misfortune during the monarchy.

Highlights in First-Temple History

Did God keep His promises made in 2 Chronicles 7? A brief survey of the history of the First Temple indicates that He certainly did.

Solomon completed and dedicated the Temple (959 B.C.).

During the reign of the wicked King Rehoboam, the Temple was raided by Pharaoh Shishak (Sheshonk I, 945–924 B.C.) who took the Temple treasure, including the shields of gold that Solomon had made (1 Kings 14:25–26).

After years of neglect due to spiritual decline during the reign of Athaliah, Joash initiated restoration and repairs on the Temple (2 Kings 12:4–16). This return to the Lord brought with it a succession of four good kings and one hundred years of the so-called golden age of Judah.

King Ahaz, after visiting a pagan Temple in Damascus, built a new altar in the court of the Temple and made modifications to the Temple furniture (2 Kings 16:10–18).

Hezekiah restored the Temple to its proper order and brought spiritual reform to the land (2 Kings 18:1–7). Although Hezekiah had been forced to hand over the Temple treasure to the Assyrians when Sennacherib demanded tribute (2 Kings 18:13–15), God sent a plague into the Assyrian camp and delivered Jerusalem. God was keeping the promise He made in 2 Chronicles 7:14.

Manasseh, Hezekiah's son, became one of the most immoral kings in the history of Judah. His defiance of God was overwhelming—even to the point of his endorsing child sacrifice. As a result, God announced coming judgment on the nation. As a last-chance plea, God sent a message by the word of Jeremiah to King Jehoiakim, descendant of Manasseh and one of Judah's last kings. Jehoiakim demonstrated his defiance of God's warning by burning the scroll containing Jeremiah's message.

In December of 588 B.C., Nebuchadnezzar, king of Babylon, laid siege to Jerusalem. The Babylonians breached the city walls in the summer of 586 B.C. after one and one-half years of siege and suffering. The city of Jerusalem, including the Temple, was looted and burned (2 Kings 25:4–10). After 373 years of Levitical ministry, the sacrifices in the Jerusalem Temple ceased. Jeremiah, who witnessed these events, reports that the bronze Temple furniture was broken up and carried back to Babylon along with the gold and silver vessels and lampstands (Jer. 52:17–23). Thousands of Judeans were forced to leave their homes and settle in Babylon. This marked the beginning of the seventy-year captivity prophesied by Jeremiah (Jer. 25:11; 29:10). During this period of judgment, the Temple lay in ruins and Jerusalem became a byword among the nations, exactly what 2 Chronicles 7:19–20 states would happen.

The Second Temple

One of the first official acts of Cyrus, after his capture of Babylon (539 B.C.), was to release the Jewish exiles. This allowed them to return to their homes and reestablish their worship centers (Ezra 1:1–4).

Beginning the Rebuilding

It was under the leadership of Sheshbazzar, whom Cyrus had appointed governor of the Persian province of Judah, that the first group of exiles set out for Jerusalem, probably in the spring of 537 B.C. The purpose of this return, according to the edict of Cyrus, was to rebuild the Jerusalem Temple, the cost of which was to be paid by the Persian treasury (Ezra 1:2; 6:4).

Arriving in Jerusalem, the returnees rebuilt the holy altar and laid the foundation of the Temple (Ezra 3:1–10). Stiff opposition from the Samaritans to the north, whom the Jews prohibited from sharing in the rebuilding project (Ezra 4:1–5), brought the work on the Temple to a halt. Sixteen years passed (536–520 B.C.) before the returned exiles once again began to rebuild the Temple.

Completing the Project

The encouragement to complete the rebuilding of the Temple came from two prophets—Haggai and Zechariah (Ezra 5:1–2). Haggai challenged the people for neglecting their spiritual priorities while spending time and money to panel their own houses (Hag. 1:4). Zechariah declared that genuine repentance was a prerequisite for future blessing (Zech. 1:1–6). The people responded and began rebuilding in earnest.

Although there was outside opposition to the rebuilding project, Darius I (522–486 B.C.) confirmed the original edict of Cyrus and gave the Jews authorization to continue their work. The Second Temple was completed in 515 B.C., and the event was celebrated by a dedication and the offering of sacrifices (Ezra 6:15–17).

The Second Temple was not as grand and glorious as Solomon's, which led to some discouragement among the people (cf. Hag. 2:3–4). But Haggai encouraged the Judeans by reminding them of God's promise of future glory and divine blessing on this house of the Lord (Hag. 2:7–9). Unfortunately, we do not have a detailed description of this Temple, as we do of Solomon's. It was no doubt patterned after Solomon's Temple with a porch, Holy Place, and Most Holy Place. Although no dimensions are given, the Second Temple was probably smaller than Solomon's (cf. Ezra 3:12; Hag. 2:3).

Remodeling by King Herod

King Herod (37–4 B.C.) sought to make a lasting impression on his kingdom through his many building projects that included cities, fortress, and villas. But Herod's crowning work was his remodeling of the Jerusalem Temple.

According to Josephus, Herod's work in the Temple began in 20–19 B.C. (*Antiquities* 20.219). The sanctuary itself *(naos)* was completed in 18–17 B.C. after one and one-half years of work (*Antiquities* 15.421). However, the work on the Temple precincts continued on for many years. Although Herod died in 4 B.C., the remodeling and refinements on the Temple area were not completed until around A.D. 62 (*Antiquities* 20.219)—eight years before it was destroyed by the Romans.

In order to accommodate a larger courtyard around the Temple area, Herod enlarged the Temple Mount by adding retaining walls and subterranean arches.[4] The southern section of the completed platform rested high above bedrock on lofty arches. The entire thirty-five-acre courtyard was surrounded by beautiful colonnaded porches. In the center of this great courtyard were the altar and sanctuary where the priests ministered. Josephus reports that the Holy Place within the Temple contained a lampstand, a table, and an altar of incense. Within the Most Holy Place, he says, "stood nothing whatever." This indicates that the ark of the covenant that disappeared at the time of the 586 B.C. destruction of Jerusalem had never been found or replaced.

This description of Herod's Temple might lead us to wonder whether it ought to be considered the Third Temple, since it is so grand in comparison with the rather humble structure built by the returning exiles. Yet from the standpoint of Jewish history, the Temple built by the returning exiles was never destroyed, nor was the Temple ministry ever interrupted during Herod's remodeling. While the Second Temple was completely remodeled by Herod, it is regarded by historians as one and the same as the Temple built by the Jewish exiles upon their return from Babylon. The Jews are thus awaiting the building of the Third Temple.

Highlights in Second-Temple History

The Second Temple stood in Jerusalem for approximately 585 years— a little over two hundred years longer than had Solomon's Temple. Once again, our brief survey of Second-Temple highlights demonstrates that God's promise in 2 Chronicles 7:14 was being upheld.

The Second Temple was completed in 515 B.C. through the leadership of Zerubbabel and the encouragement of Haggai and Zechariah. The event was celebrated by a dedication and the offering of sacrifices (Ezra 6:15–17).

The Temple ministry was enhanced through the work of Ezra, the scribe, who came to Jerusalem in 458 B.C. Operating under the authority of Artaxerxes (464–424 B.C.), Ezra presented offerings of silver and gold in the Temple, assigned duties to the Levites, and taught the people the law (Ezra 7:12–26).

Antiochus IV (175–163 B.C.) made his name in history as the infamous ruler of Syria who proclaimed himself "Ephiphanes" (the manifest god) and sought to enforce the worship of Zeus in Jerusalem. On December 16, 167 B.C., the Second Temple was dedicated to the worship of Zeus and a pig was sacrificed on the great altar (1 Macc. 1:29–67).

The desecration of the Temple by Antiochus was not to be ignored. During those days, some resisted heroically, led and inspired as they were by the Maccabees (cf. 1 Macc. 2). After three years of fighting, Judas Maccabeus and his soldiers were able to capture the Temple Mount. On December 14, 164 B.C., the Temple was cleansed from the defilement of pagan worship and sacrifices were offered on a newly built altar. The rededication of the Temple is commemorated by the Jews at an annual festival known as Hanukkah ("dedication").

The Roman Empire gradually expanded and eventually annexed the entire eastern Mediterranean region. In 63 B.C. the Roman general Pompey marched on Jerusalem. When the Romans breached the walls and invaded the Temple, the priests continued their ministry as if nothing had happened. According to Josephus, Pompey and some of his men entered the sanctuary (*Antiquities* 14.71–72). However, they did not touch the Temple or its treasures. On the next day, the Levites cleansed the Temple and continued the customary sacrifices.

Herod began remodeling the Temple in 20–19 B.C. (*Antiquities* 20.219) and completed the sanctuary *(naos)* after one and one-half years of work (*Antiquities* 15.421). The work on the Temple complex was not completed until long after Herod's death, around A.D. 62 (*Antiquities*, 20.219).

The Second Temple was destroyed by the Romans in A.D. 70 after four years of revolt against Roman tyranny (A.D. 66–70). The Romans breached the outer walls of Jerusalem in late May A.D. 70 and began to penetrate the city. On August 6, sacrifice ceased in the Jerusalem Temple. The porches of the Temple were burned on August 15–17. After a ramp was raised against the inner wall, the sanctuary was entered and burned on the ninth of Av, about August 28. This was the same day that the First Temple had been burned by the Babylonians (Josephus *War* 6.250).

The Present Temple

We noted earlier that the Temple carries a message of God's redemption. The furniture of the Temple and its ceremonies all point to God's redemptive work as culminated in Christ. Today there is no Temple standing on Mount Moriah in Jerusalem. Does that mean that the message of the Temple—the picture of God and His redemptive work—has vanished from this earth as well?

The answer to this question is found in 1 Corinthians 6:19, where the apostle Paul makes a startling declaration, "Or do you not know that your body is a temple of the Holy Spirit who is in you, whom you have from God, and that you are not your own?" The word for *temple* is the Greek word *naos,* which means "the dwelling of God."

Those who have become believers in Jesus Christ have become God's Temple. Believers in Christ are God's representation of what the Temple was designed to communicate to humanity.

As Christians, we must consider how well we represent the message of God's Temple. Do our lives depict something of the nature of God's holy Temple? Does the Temple of my body exemplify a clean and pure life? Does my life show that I receive my spiritual sustenance from God? Do I live in such a way to show that God's light is in my life?

We have considered its beginnings under King Solomon. We have traced its history through the Old Testament and into the New Testament period. The Temple is a theme that ties the Bible together from beginning to end—the presence of God among His people forever.

Endnotes

1. Scholars have established that the unit used in measuring the Temple was the royal cubit, about twenty-one inches. This is also called a cubit and a handbreadth.
2. It is not clear from the biblical text whether the olive wood doors took the place of the veil or were in addition to the veil.
3. This may sound impressive until we note that Solomon spent thirteen years building his own house (1 Kings 7:1).
4. Josephus provides a very helpful description of the Jerusalem Temple (*War* 5.184–227).

3

Ezekiel:
The Prophet of Israel's
Future Temple

The prophet Ezekiel provides us with a description of the future Temple—its dimensions, altar, and sacrifices. But who is Ezekiel? He remains one of the least known prophets of the Bible. When we ask people about Ezekiel, they usually say something about dry bones. Well, there is more to Ezekiel than dry bones! We have found him to be one of the most unusual and interesting prophets of the Bible. In this chapter we would like you to get acquainted with Ezekiel, the prophet of Israel's future Temple.

Ezekiel might be best remembered as the prophet of pantomime because of his extensive use of this technique. The mind of the Hebrews was much more given to receiving truth through symbols than is our Western analytical mind. This is why many of the prophets used symbolic actions when communicating divine revelation. For example, Isaiah walked naked for three years (Isa. 20:1–6). Jeremiah wore a yoke around his neck (Jer. 27–28). Hosea married a "wife of harlotry" (Hos. 1–3). But Ezekiel excelled them all in his use of symbolic actions. Being a priest by upbringing and training, symbolism on a grand scale was second nature to him, especially symbolism that combined word and deed.

For Ezekiel, everything had a message. His dramatic actions, later combined with words, were a powerful means of communicating God's revelation to God's people. Ezekiel's symbolic actions had an even greater impact because he was mute during the first seven and a half years of his ministry.

The prophet Ezekiel could not speak—unless God chose to speak a message through him. Ezekiel could not say, "Dear, please serve me some more of that unleavened bread," or "What's new in the *Jerusalem Times*?" He could only say, "Thus says the Lord. . . ."

To carry on his ministry, Ezekiel would walk to the city center and begin his pantomime. You can imagine how the people must have gathered around and wondered, *What is he up to today?* They would probably question each other and debate the meaning. When the symbolic action was finally complete, Ezekiel would return home. Later, the city elders would come to his house saying, "OK, Ezekiel, what is God saying?" Then Ezekiel would declare, "Thus says the Lord. . . ." And the prophet of pantomime would explain the symbolic action.

The Times of Ezekiel

Ezekiel's world of symbolism and pantomime may have been different from our Western world, but in many respects the political climate in which Ezekiel lived parallels our world today. At the end of the seventh century B.C. three powers were vying for control over the Middle East—Assyria, Babylonia, and Egypt. These powerful nations were constantly at war with one another. They were using the small state of Israel as a major highway to move from their own borders to the next battlefield.

It is interesting to note that the situation has not changed that much since biblical times. Egypt, Jordan, Syria, Iraq, and Iran all recognize the importance of having access to Israel's territory. Many wars and peace agreements in the Middle East have focused on this one issue.

In 605 B.C., the Babylonians fought with the Egyptians at Carchemish over the control of Syria and the Holy Land. The Egyptians were defeated, and Babylon became the new world power. Nebuchadnezzar, king of Babylon, moved quickly to take possession of his newly won territory of Judah. He proceeded to Jerusalem and took some of the royal family, along with many Temple vessels, back to Babylon (Dan. 1:1–3). This was the first of three Jewish captivities in Babylon.

Ezekiel would have been a young man at the time of the first captivity. He was busy training for the priesthood. He sometimes may have doubted whether he would have the opportunity to fulfill the demands of his office. The Babylonians had a well-established pattern of capturing nations and deporting their citizens to a foreign land. He probably wondered if he would be among the next group of Jews exiled from the land.

Ezekiel did not have long to wait to discover his destiny. It was 597 B.C. and Jehoiachin had been ruling Judah for three months when Nebuchadnezzar marched on Jerusalem and besieged the city. The king and his family were captured and exiled to Babylon. The royal and Temple treasures were pillaged. Ten thousand Judeans—the best of the craftsmen and smiths—were deported to Babylon. Ezekiel was among them.

Ezekiel's Training for the Priesthood

Ezekiel had spent a good part of his life in training for the priesthood. The training of priests was a serious and rigorous matter—a violation of specified ritual could cost the priest his life as it had the sons of Aaron (cf. Lev. 10:1–3). What did Ezekiel's priestly training involve?

First of all, a priest would be trained in the exact details and specifications for Temple ministry. The priests were trained in how to offer a sacrifice, burn incense, trim the lamps, prepare the showbread, and officiate on feast days. Priests would be trained in the slaughter of sacrificial animals. They were shown how to kill and butcher the animal so that its suffering was minimal and the carcass would be drained of blood. They were also trained in the culinary arts so they could mix the grain offering and bake the showbread.

Second, the priest would be trained in matters of health. Priests were responsible to inspect those suspected of having leprosy (Lev. 13:1–3). On the basis of the priests' examination, an Israelite would be pronounced "clean" or "unclean." Furthermore, the priests had the authority to inspect and quarantine a house that had the mark of leprosy (Lev. 14:34).

A third area of priestly training would be in the area of law and justice. The priests were responsible to know the law and to teach the law to God's people. Ezra, for example, was a priest who was skilled in the law of Moses (Ezra 7:6) and gave himself to teaching God's Word to Israel (Ezra 7:10, 25). Priests were also responsible to mediate certain judicial proceedings, such as when a wife was accused of adultery (cf. Num. 5:11–31). The priests acted as a high court of appeals in difficult cases. The judicial aspect of priestly training would also have included law enforcement in the Temple area. Recall how Jeremiah, and later Paul, were arrested in the Temple area by Temple police.

Fourth, priests were also trained in financial administration. The business and financial aspects of the Temple ministry have been often overlooked. The Temple was big business. Millions and millions of shekels came into the Temple treasury annually. The priests were responsible to collect these offerings, count the money, designate the funds to various accounts, and distribute the priests' stipends.

Fifth, some priests were trained in construction and maintenance.

Remember, only priests could enter the Temple. If the ceiling needed repair or a piece of Temple furniture needed refinishing, it was the priests who would carry out these duties.

Finally, some priests were trained as musicians to prepare music for worship and celebration. Music and singing were important dimensions of worship in ancient Israel. Some priests were trained as trumpeters (2 Chron. 5:12–13); others were trained as worship leaders (Neh. 8:4–8). Together with the Levites and the community of Israel, they gave praise to the Lord.

As a priest in training, Ezekiel would have studied all these areas, most likely specializing in one area or another. For years he had been studying the sacrifices, the altar, and the Temple. He had learned about the sacrificial rituals and the exact specifications for performing priestly ministry. Now, however, he was an exile. He would have no opportunity to use his training at the Temple. Or would he?

Although Ezekiel did not know it at the time, his priestly training was not going to be wasted. God was going to give His people a description of a future Temple. To do this God needed someone who was very familiar with the Temple and its ministry. Ezekiel was just the man whom God could use to communicate the vision of the Temple. His familiarity with the Temple and its ritual would be a key asset in his understanding and recording the vision of Israel's future Temple.

There is an encouraging lesson for us here. God can and will use the somewhat unusual circumstances of our lives. Ezekiel's training for the priesthood was not wasted. God had a plan for Ezekiel that was beyond his wildest dreams.

Ezekiel's Vision of the Wheels (Ezek. 1:4–28)

Ezekiel was thirty years old when he received his first vision. This was the age for a priest in Israel to begin his public ministry (Num. 4:23, 30). Ezekiel was living at the Jewish community of Tel-abib, located on the river Chebar, a navigable canal linked to the Euphrates, about twenty-five miles south of Babylon.

The Bible records that Ezekiel's vision of the wheels took place in the fifth year of the captivity, or 593 B.C. (Ezek. 1:2). As he was watching the horizon, Ezekiel saw a storm cloud approaching. It must have been something like an electrical storm, for there was lightning flashing from the cloud. Within the approaching cloud, Ezekiel noticed that there were four living creatures, later identified as cherubim (10:20), angelic guardians of God's holiness. Each had a human form, four wings and four faces—those of a man, a lion, an ox, and an eagle.

Ezekiel noticed that the living creatures were associated with four wheels. The wheels were arranged in such a way so as to make it appear that one wheel was within the other (Ezek. 1:16). The wheels sparkled like precious stones and had what appeared to be eyes along the rims (1:18). The wheels were able to move in any direction without turning. They followed the movements of the living creatures.

Above the living creatures there was a great expanse—something like a cloud with the gleam of crystal. And over the gleaming expanse, Ezekiel saw the likeness of a man seated on a marine-blue throne. The figure on the throne had the appearance of glowing metal, and he was surrounded by a radiance like that of a rainbow.

What is the meaning of Ezekiel's vision? There are about as many differing interpretations as there are commentaries. We suggest that most commentators have read their ideas into this vision rather than simply taking the interpretation offered by Ezekiel himself. In verse 1, Ezekiel explains that his eyes were opened and he saw visions of God. In verse 28, he reports that his vision portrayed the "likeness of the glory of the LORD." Ezekiel's first vision was simply a vision of the glory of God. Instead of trying to interpret the minute details, we need to respond with our hearts and emotions as Ezekiel did. We need to fall on our faces and listen to the voice of God.

Ezekiel Called As a Prophet (Ezek. 2:1–3:11)

Like Isaiah, Ezekiel was called to prophesy to a rebellious people who would not want to listen. In verse 1, Ezekiel is addressed by the term *son of man.* This designation, used ninety-three times in the book, basically means "mortal man." The term expresses human weakness in the presence of God's majesty and power.

Although Ezekiel was being sent by the Lord to minister to a people characterized by the words *stubborn, obstinate,* and *rebellious,* he is charged by the Lord to neither "fear them nor their words" (Ezek. 2:6). Ezekiel is charged by the Lord to speak His words "whether they listen or not" (2:7).

It is significant to note that the success of Ezekiel's ministry would not be measured by how well the people responded to his message. Ezekiel was told from the beginning of his ministry that the people would not listen. His success would be measured by his faithfulness in proclaiming God's message.

God never sends a messenger without a message. Before Ezekiel begins his prophetic ministry, he must assimilate God's message, which he will then proclaim to others. This is symbolically portrayed in Ezekiel 2:8–3:3. Ezekiel is shown a scroll that contains lamentations, mourning, and woe (2:10). It is clear that the scroll contains a message of judgment.

Then Ezekiel is commanded, "Son of man, eat what you find; eat this scroll, and go, speak to the house of Israel" (Ezek. 3:1). Ezekiel did as he was instructed. He opened his mouth and God fed him the scroll. The eating of the scroll is a picture of Ezekiel's need to assimilate the divine message that he is to deliver to the people. Someone has said, "You cannot feed others spiritually until you have fed yourself." When he ate the scroll, Ezekiel discovered that it tasted as sweet as honey. Although it contained a message of judgment, the scroll was sweet because it was the Word of God (cf. Ps. 19:10).

Ezekiel is called by God to minister without ever expecting a response. God declares that it would be easier to learn a foreign language and deliver his message to a foreign nation than to penetrate the stubborn deafness of Israel (Ezek. 3:5–6). It is rather significant that language barriers can be more easily overcome than the spiritual hindrance of an unresponsive heart. To meet the challenge for this difficult ministry, God gave Ezekiel a head as hard as the hearts of the people (3:9).

Once again, Ezekiel is told that he must go and speak to the people whether they listen or not (Ezek. 3:11; cf. 2:5). There is a good application for us here. God has called us to share the gospel—the Good News of Jesus Christ. We are responsible to deliver the message no matter how people respond.

Appointed As a Watchman (Ezek. 3:12–21)

The next thing Ezekiel realized after receiving his call was that the Spirit of the Lord had lifted him up! He heard the sound of the wings of the cherubim and the rumbling of the wheels as he departed. Then he found himself among the exiles who lived beside the river Chebar at Tel-abib, a major settlement of the Jewish exiles in Babylon (Ezek. 3:15).

Ezekiel began his prophetic ministry not by speaking, but with seven days of silence. The words he was to speak caused him "consternation" (Ezek. 3:15). It may be better rendered that Ezekiel "showed horror." This may suggest that Ezekiel was overwhelmed or stunned as he contemplated the challenge that was before him.

At the end of the seven days the Lord spoke again to Ezekiel. In verse

17 the Lord declares that Ezekiel has been appointed a watchman to the house of Israel. In ancient times a watchman was responsible to stand on the city wall and look out over the roads approaching the gates (2 Sam. 18:24–27; 2 Kings 9:17–20). If an enemy should approach, he would call down an order for the gates to be shut and barred. The watchman would also be responsible to watch for messengers or couriers who might be bringing good news to the city. The watchman would herald the messenger's approach and assure him a welcome. Watchmen were also positioned on watch towers in the fields during harvest. They were to watch over the property and make sure the ripening crops were not stolen before they could be harvested.

Ezekiel was appointed a watchman to the people of Israel. As a watchman, he was responsible to warn them of the imminent danger of divine judgment. He was to warn the wicked of their need to repent (Ezek. 3:16–19) and warn the righteous that if they turned to sin, they would face judgment (3:20–21). Ezekiel is reminded that he is accountable for the faithful deliverance of the message, not the success or failure of the response. If he failed to do his duty, Ezekiel would be held accountable (3:18, 20).

Restrained in His Ministry (Ezek. 3:22–27)

The commissioning of Ezekiel concludes with another vision of God's glory (Ezek. 3:23). Once again, Ezekiel fell on his face before the Lord (cf. 1:28). Then the Spirit of the Lord told Ezekiel, "Go shut yourself up in your house" (3:24). This indicates that Ezekiel was to withdraw from public life and carry out his prophetic ministry from his home. Although he would exhibit symbolic actions in public, he would return home afterward. The elders of the community would then go to Ezekiel's home to consult him privately (cf. Ezek. 8:1, 14:1, 20:1). Then he would declare, "Thus says the Lord," and proclaim God's message for the people.

Not only would Ezekiel remain mainly at home, but verse 25 indicates that he would be "bound with ropes" so that he could not go out among the people. The binding of the prophet probably signifies his rejection by his people (cf. Ezek. 2:5; 3:7). The binding of Ezekiel is probably also literal. This may have resulted from attempts by the Jewish leaders to restrain a prophet who seems to have gone mad.

A third rather limiting factor to Ezekiel's ministry is that he would be mute—unable to speak—unless the Lord opened his mouth to proclaim His Word (Ezek. 3:26–27). This unusual condition continued for the first seven and one-half years of Ezekiel's ministry. After the fall of Jerusalem in 586 B.C., he was restored to full speaking abilities (cf. 33:22). He used the rest of his days to bring words of comfort and encouragement to God's people.

Ezekiel's Symbolic Actions (Ezek. 4–24)

Chapters 4–24 record how Ezekiel used numerous symbolic actions to make God's message known to His people. These pantomimes attracted attention, raised questions, and caused people to ponder their meaning. Later, after Ezekiel completed his minidrama, the people would consult with the city elders, and the elders would go to Ezekiel. There in his home, Ezekiel's tongue was loosened by the Lord, and he was free to declare the meaning of his actions and drive home the application. We will highlight a few of Ezekiel's symbolic actions.

The Sign of the Brick (Ezek. 4:1–3)

In his first symbolic action, Ezekiel is commanded to inscribe a map of Jerusalem on a soft clay brick. He is then commanded to "lay siege against it." Apparently he built a small siege wall around the brick, with ramps, camps, and battering rams. This symbolic action served to forewarn the Israelites of the coming siege of Jerusalem.

The Sign of the Prophet's Posture (Ezek. 4:4–8)

In the next symbolic action, Ezekiel was commanded to lie on his left side for 390 days and on his right side for 40 days. Verse 5 makes it clear that each day represents a year during which the nation would bear judgment for her past sins.

The Sign of Famine (Ezek. 4:9–17)

Scarcity of food is one of the great horrors of military siege. Ezekiel was commanded to eat a daily ration of about nine ounces of bread and a quart of water. He baked the bread in the sight of the people, using cow manure to fuel the fire.

The Sign of the Knife and Razor (Ezek. 5:1–17)

Ezekiel was commanded to shave his head and beard with a sharp sword. The hair, which represented the Israelite people, was to be divided into three portions. The first part was to be burned with fire; the second to be cut with the sword; and the third part was to be scattered to the wind.

The Sign of the Baggage (Ezek. 12:1–16)

Ezekiel was commanded to pack his bags and carry them out of his house as if he were going on a journey. The fact is, the people of Judah were going on a journey—a journey into exile.

The Sign of the Signpost (Ezek. 21:18–20)

God commanded Ezekiel to make a signpost with an arrow pointing to Jerusalem and another to Ammon. The king of Babylon is pictured as standing at the fork of the road trying to determine which to take. He decided to go to Jerusalem first.

The Sign of Ezekiel's Wife (Ezek. 24:15–27)

When Jerusalem fell under siege in December of 588 B.C., God revealed to Ezekiel that his wife was soon to die. The prophet was then commanded not to mourn or weep. He could groan silently but was to display no outward emotion over his wife's death. His actions were a sign to the people of Jerusalem that they were not to mourn the destruction of their city since it came as the result of divine judgment.

Ezekiel's New Beginning

When the report of Jerusalem's fall reached the ears of Ezekiel, the Lord did an amazing thing. Ezekiel's tongue was loosed and he began to speak freely (Ezek. 24:25–27). The miraculous release of his tongue was another sign that God was speaking through Ezekiel and that his claims were true.

Jerusalem had been destroyed and the Temple had been burned, but Ezekiel's tongue was now freed to speak messages of comfort and hope to his people. Much comfort and encouragement has been found in his prophecy that God is going to raise up another glorious Temple.

4

Attempts at Rebuilding the Temple

June 7, 1967, was a historic day for Jerusalem and the Jewish people. It was on that day during the Six-Day War that Israeli paratroopers broke through the St. Stephens Gate to liberate the Old City of Jerusalem and capture the Temple Mount.

A young Israeli soldier was at this most holy site of Jerusalem on the evening of June 7. On crutches because he had been wounded in earlier fighting, this soldier stood on the grounds of the Temple Mount and pondered the events that had brought him to this moment. His mind and heart were filled to overflowing with emotion. For two thousand years Jews had waited for the opportunity to once again control the Temple Mount and reestablish Temple worship. His father and grandfather had died before seeing this day. He had almost died, as other soldiers had. By divine providence, however, he was only wounded.

And now, here he was on the Temple Mount. Earlier that day he had been with the troops as they entered the Dome of the Rock, a place where many believe that the Temple once stood. There he saw many Israeli soldiers crying tears of joy. Among those weeping were Jewish men who were not religious but were crying with the rest. This young soldier asked his comrades, "Why do you cry? You are not religious." They replied, "We have never felt so close to God as we do at this moment."

There on the Temple Mount, the night of June 7, was a young Jordanian official who had served as an official guide at the Muslim shrine, the Dome of the Rock. During the course of the evening, the Israeli struck up a conversation with the Jordanian. They talked of many things.

Then the young guide said, "We know in a few days you will be rebuilding your Temple. So, just to save you the trouble, let me show you where it stood." He pointed to the Dome of the Rock. "There," he explained, "was where Solomon and later Herod built their Temples!"

After two thousand years of Gentile domination, God once again allowed His chosen people to enter the Golden City and bring it under Israeli control. Soldiers who had fought their way through the Old City and onto the Temple Mount stood in awe as one of their number scaled the Dome of the Rock and placed an Israeli flag on top of it! A cry of joy sprang from the troops as they entered the Dome of the Rock. But their cries of joy turned to quiet prayers of gratitude to God as they worshiped where their ancestors had worshiped years ago. As the Temple platform filled with Jewish soldiers, it seemed clear to all that God had given the Temple Mount back to His people.

The Six-Day War came to an end and negotiations between Israel and the Palestinians began. The world looked on in astonishment, and many Jews in horror, as the Israeli government performed an ultimate act of conciliation. They returned the Dome of the Rock to Arab hands. The young Jordanian and the wounded Israeli soldier were among those who could not believe what they were hearing and seeing. How could they come so close to once again having a Temple and then allow it to slip through their fingers? Two Jewish soldiers, unknown to each other at the time, both vowed that never again would Israel come this close to having a Temple and the nation not be ready to rebuild.

Gershon Salomon, the young Israeli soldier, would eventually enter politics, serve in the administration of Menachem Begin, and serve on the city council of Jerusalem. But his most significant accomplishment was the founding of an organization known as the Temple Mount Faithful.

Rabbi Yisrael Ariel, another soldier on the Temple Mount that evening, went on to establish a rabbinical study center, the Temple Institute. He has given his life to the preparation of ritual implements for use in the next Temple.

Shortly after the Six-Day War, several rabbis met in the home of Rabbi Nachman Kahanna and began what was to become Israel's Temple movement. At the same time, across Jerusalem, another group got together. Their association is called *Ateret Kohanannim,* meaning "royal priesthood." This organization was founded in order to train young Israelis who have the proper historical lineage for the priesthood. Nachman Kahanna would later become the leader of another school also training men for the priesthood. Over the years, these organizations, along with another group founded by Chief Rabbi Shlomo Goren, have trained thousands of Jewish men who will be able to immediately begin priestly functions should the Temple worship begin tomorrow.

The Sanhedrin Institute, directed by Torah scholar Yoel Lerner, is dedicated to studying the Talmud and Torah so as to learn about the Sanhedrin, the ruling body by which the Temple is operated. There is even a room set up for the Sanhedrin today in the vicinity of the Temple area.

A Historical Perspective

Ever since the Jerusalem Temple was destroyed, there have been those who have worked and hoped for its rebuilding. Rabbi Yohannan Ben Zakkai witnessed the last days of the Jerusalem Temple and was a key leader in the formulation of what Judaism would be without a Temple. Yet, he taught that priests should keep track of the day they would have had assigned duties in the Temple service and should conduct themselves on those days according to the same regulations applicable during the existence of the Temple. This meant that the priests should not drink wine on such days in order to remain in a state of preparedness should they be called on to exercise their priestly duties.[1] This ruling helped create and maintain a sense of expectation and readiness for the rebuilding of the Temple.

Rabbi Yehoshua Ben Chananya

The Talmud records that a few short years after the destruction of the Temple by the Romans in A.D. 70, the Jews made their first attempt at rebuilding. Fundraising for the project was well under way when the Samaritans warned the emperor that the Jews were rebuilding their Temple with plans to rebel. The Roman emperor Hadrian (117–38) responded with a decree that caused the Jews to cry and wail. They considered rebelling against Hadrian, but were warned by Rabbi Yehoshua Ben Chananya against this course of action. "It is enough," he said, "that we have escaped from these people with our lives" (*Bereshit Rabbah*, 64). The Jews then dispersed and reluctantly returned home.

Bar Kokhba's Rebellion

When the Jews learned that Hadrian had decided to erect a Roman Temple on the site of the holy Temple, a rebellion erupted, which has become known by the name of its leader, Bar Kokhba. The rebuilding of the Jerusalem Temple was one of the chief objectives of Bar Kokhba and his rebel followers. The fighters gained in strength and eventually took control of Jerusalem and its vicinity. It is unclear, however, whether the fighters were able to achieve their objective of renewing the Temple service.

The revolt was put down by Hadrian in 135, and Jerusalem was rebuilt as a Roman city and named Aelia Capitolina. *Aelia* was Hadrian's middle name, and *Capitolina* refers to the god Jupiter Capitolinus. Where the Jewish Temple once stood, Hadrian erected a Temple to Jupiter and a statue of himself. Thus, this first effort to rebuild the Jerusalem Temple was thwarted.

Moses ben Maimon

There is probably no other rabbi who has had a more profound and lasting influence on the development of Jewish theology than Moses ben Maimon, more commonly known as Maimonides. He was born in Cordova, Spain, in 1135 and died in Cairo in 1204, having lived out his days as a learned teacher and philosopher. One of his greatest accomplishments was to write a complete commentary on the Mishnah.[2] He also wrote a commentary on the Torah that was to contain all that a faithful Jew must know, so that he need not spend his entire time in Talmudic controversies and disputations. In his classic work, *Book of the Commandments*, Maimonides explains the details of each commandment. One of the commandments recognized and expounded by the great teacher was the commandment to rebuild the Temple. Maimonides explains:

> The Creator commanded us to erect a chosen House for His service, where the sacrificial offerings will be brought . . . for all time . . . , this commandment is general and includes many details: the menorah, the table, the altar, etc.—these are all intrinsic parts of the Temple . . . and all of the detailed ordinances of this commandment including the construction and its design are all explained in the tractate which was compiled for this purpose, tractate *Middot*" (*The Book of Commandments,* 20).

There are three main points that Maimonides makes in this discussion. First, the purpose of the commandment to build the Temple is to offer sacrifices. Second, the vessels of the Temple are an intrinsic part of the commandment and constitute a portion of the Temple structure. Third, the accepted design of the future Temple is that which is described in the tractate *Middot* of the Babylonian Talmud.[3] These teachings are universally accepted as legally binding by great Torah scholars since medieval times.

The Tosafists

Over the centuries, various attempts have been made by Jewish people to reestablish the Temple. One of the noteworthy efforts took place in the time of the "Tosafists," the French school of Torah scholars comprised of the descendants and disciples of the famous medieval commentator, Rabbi Shlomo Ben Yitzchak, known by the name Rashi. During this time, a large number of French Jews were migrating to Israel. One of these Jewish immigrants, Rabbi Yechiel of Paris (d. 1268), began making preparations for the resumption of the Temple service.

About this time, Rabbi Ashtori HaParchi discussed the rebuilding of the Temple with his master, Rabbi Baruch of Jerusalem, and came to some significant conclusions. Two questions were prominent in his thinking:

1. Is it possible to begin Temple services while Israel is in a state of impurity? Rabbi HaParchi concluded that congregational sacrifices (pertaining to the entire nation) take precedence over impurity and override it.

2. May only the priests who possess pedigree documents, which trace their lineage and establish their priesthood, perform Temple service? Rabbi HaParchi maintained that any individual who has a family tradition of priestly service may serve in the Temple even if he does not possess a document.

During this period, many Jewish scholars in France immigrated to the Holy Land. They settled in Jerusalem, Acre, and other cities. Struggles and persecutions eventually slowed the Tosafists' movement and the objective of rebuilding the Temple was never realized.

Pre-1948 Developments

In the 1800s there was a growing interest among European Jews as to the possibility of renewing national life in their homeland. Many were interested as well in the rebuilding of the Jerusalem Temple. Rabbi Zevi Hirsch Kalisher, a German Jew, was a leading figure in this effort. Kalisher, a prolific writer, took an active interest in the plight of homeless eastern

Jews. He wrote a book, *Derosjat Ziyyon,* in which he proposed to collect money from Jewish people to purchase and cultivate land in Palestine. His book contained three theses: (1) the salvation of the Jews can come about only by self-help, (2) the colonization of Palestine is necessary to provide a home for homeless Jews, and (3) the sacrificial system of the Temple should be reestablished. To accomplish this objective Kalisher sought to persuade the great Jewish philanthropist Baron Asher Anshil Rothschild to purchase the entire land of Israel from Ibrahim Pasha, king of Egypt, who ruled over the Holy Land at the time. He suggested to Baron Rothschild that if Pasha refused to sell the whole land, then he could at least be persuaded to sell Jerusalem and the Temple Mount.

In his letter to Rothschild, Rabbi Kalisher explained how a renewal of the Temple service would lead to mass immigration of the Jewish people to the land of Israel. He insisted that the obligation to rebuild the Jerusalem Temple and renew Temple service applies in every generation—especially in a time when there was a chance for a Jewish government in Jerusalem. Although his efforts did not meet with immediate success, Kalisher never lost hope of seeing the Temple rebuilt. He is considered one of the most important rabbis who prepared the way for modern Zionism.

Modern Temple Movements

Since the reestablishment of the nation of Israel as a Jewish state in 1948, there has been increased interest in rebuilding the Temple in Jerusalem. It is indeed thrilling to see Jewish people actively laboring for what may become the fulfillment of biblical prophecy.

Research Center for Jewish Thought

In 1984 seven Israeli scholars met to discuss the possibility of putting together the information needed to bring Israel's legal system into proper alignment for Temple worship and procedures. This organization eventually became known as the Sanhedrin Institute. The name was later changed to the Research Center for Jewish Thought. Today the Research Center is under the direction of Yoel Lerner.

The organization's stated purpose is to assure that when a Temple is built, the laws necessary to connect the Temple to civilian life will already be in place. Their first publication, *The Manual on Punishment and Rehabilitation of Criminals in Jewish Life,* appeared in 1986. Since then six other documents have been written. Two relate to the status of minors and their rights. Three address issues of the constitution, rabbinical courts,

Torah scholar Yoel Lerner of the Research Center for Jewish Thought (formerly called the Sanhedren Institute) discusses temple location information with John.

and human rights as they relate to the Temple worship. The remaining publication is a proposed constitution allowing for the inclusion of Temple worship in the public life of Israel.

Since 1984, the organization has been publishing a magazine whose articles discuss issues of the Temple and its relationship to civil law. Courses are being offered by the Center to help the general public become aware of the changes in civil law that will be necessary to incorporate a Temple into Israel's existence.

Temple Mount Faithful

An organization called the Temple Mount Faithful was established on the fourth day of Israel's Six Day War in 1967. Those participating in the initial meetings included Gershon Salomon, Zeev Bar Tove, Rabbi Moshe Sagal, Rabbi Levi Isaac Rabinovich, and Professor Israel Eldod. It was clear to these men that the capture of the Temple Mount was not just an outcome of war but evidence of the hand of God in Israel's destiny. Their purpose in establishing the Temple Mount Faithful organization was to educate and convince the people of Israel that building the next Temple is the will of God. The infant organization also sought to convince government leaders that the capture of the Temple Mount was an

Gershon Salomon and Zeev Bar Tove, leaders of the Temple Mount Faithful, discussing the temple model with John.

indication that it was time to reestablish the Temple. At that time, the Israeli government refused to acknowledge their pleas and gave the Temple Mount back to the Arabs. To the leaders of the Temple Mount Faithful, this was an indication that the nation was not yet ready for the next Temple. It is their desire that the nation of Israel will be ready for the Temple the next time they have such an opportunity.

The Temple Mount Faithful continues efforts to influence the Israeli government to acknowledge Israel's right to the Temple Mount. They have also been involved in influencing the general public in Israel as to the importance of following God's Word instead of secular opinion. One of their major objectives is to unite the people of Israel in prayer, especially on holy days, directing these prayers toward the Temple Mount.

The Temple Mount Faithful have in their possession a stone that they intend to use as the cornerstone for the Third Temple. The stone was found in the Negev and shows evidence of having been worked by human hands. It is known that the stones of the Temple were taken by the Romans into the Negev for disposal. According to tradition, when Herod remodeled the Temple, extra stones and rejected stones were also taken to the Negev. The stone designated as the future cornerstone may have a connection with the previous Temple as one of the rejected stones. This being the

John discussing the Temple of Ezekiel with Rabbi Yisrael Ariel and Rabbi Chaim Richman, leading rabbis of the Temple Institute in Jerusalem.

case, the stone in the possession of the Temple Mount Faithful may relate to Psalm 118:22, "The stone which the builders rejected has become the chief cornerstone." This is primarily a prophecy concerning the rejection of Jesus, the Messiah. It would be ironic if a stone rejected by the builders of the Second Temple became the cornerstone of the Third Temple.

The Temple Institute

The spiritual leader of the Temple Institute is Rabbi Yisrael Ariel. He was one of the first Israeli soldiers to reach the Temple Mount after the capture of the Old City of Jerusalem in 1967. Leaders of the Institute believe that their task is "to advance the cause of the Temple and to prepare for its establishment, not just talk about it."[4]

Chaim Richman, spokesman for the Temple Institute, elaborates on the purpose of the organization:

> The goal of our Institute is to raise the consciousness first and foremost of the Jewish people and of the world at large to the spiritual realization that the vacuum of spiritual fulfillment which all of man suffers from today can only be fulfilled by the establishment of a holy Temple in Jerusalem.[5]

During the years since the founding of the Temple Institute, more than half of the ninety-three ritual implements necessary for priestly functions have been constructed. Among the prized items are a priestly crown made of one hundred grams of pure gold inscribed with the words *Holy to God.* There is also a six-pound silver container called a *mizrak* that will be used to collect the sacrificial blood and pour it out at the altar. Other items will be prepared as funds permit. The completed items are on display at the Temple Institute's museum in the Jewish Quarter.

Although the Temple Institute is not involved with training for the priesthood, Richman reports that there are a number of Yeshivot (rabbinical schools) that are engaged in the study of the relevant sections of Jewish law that pertain to priestly ministry in the Temple.

Rabbi Shlomo Goren

Another key player in advancing the cause of Israel's next Temple was Chief Rabbi Shlomo Goren. The late rabbi believed that he had determined the exact location of the Holy of Holies of the ancient Temple. He also had evidence that led him to believe that the ark of the covenant and the golden menorah were hidden on the Temple Mount below the Holy of Holies. For him this meant that Jews could go up to the Temple Mount for prayer without fear of desecrating this holy place. In 1989, Goren said, "I cannot leave this world without assuring that Jews will once again pray on the Mount."[6] Rabbi Goren died in November 1994, before the full realization of his dream. Yet the rabbi left behind many followers who are committed to seeing his dream become a reality.

The Future Temple Today

What is the current state of affairs regarding the future Temple? At this time, two Yeshivas, or Talmudic schools, in Jerusalem are teaching students the elaborate details of Temple service. Temple implements necessary for the ritual of sacrifice are being prepared. Reliable sources indicate that there are current efforts in Israel to breed an unblemished "red heifer"[7] so that its ashes can be prepared for the ritual cleansing of those entering the Temple area (cf. Num. 19:1–10). Priestly garments are being prepared from spun flax according to scriptural specifications (Exod. 39:1–31).

One frequently hears rumors that a group in Israel is secretly stockpiling limestone and marble to build the Temple. These rumors are unfounded. Yet Gershom Solomon and his Temple Faithful have set up a foundation stone for the Temple. Because of political consideration, the stone is not on the Temple platform. It rests today at the U.S. Consulate in East Jerusalem. Maybe someday it will be found on the Temple site.

Jewish historian David Solomon insists that a new Jewish Temple is essential. He says, "It was the essence of our Jewish being, the unifying force of our people."[8] Other Jewish people reject the literal interpretation of Scripture that leads many to expect the rebuilding of the Temple. And so the debate continues.

Those who are hopeful and expectant regarding the rebuilding of the Jerusalem Temple admit that it may be a long time before construction actually begins. Zev Golan, representing the Temple Institute, acknowledges, "No one can say how, and no one wants to do it by force. But sooner or later, in a week or in a century, it will be done. And we will be ready for it."[9]

Endnotes

1. Rabbi Yisrael Ariel, *The Odyssey of the Third Temple,* translated and adapted by Chaim Richman (Jerusalem: G. Israel Publications and Productions Ltd. and the Temple Institute, 1994), 68–69.
2. The Mishnah is a literary record of four centuries of Jewish religious thought and cultural activity in Palestine from about 150 B.C. to A.D. 200. It contains the Jewish traditions that were observed during the time of Jesus.
3. The last point marks a crucial difference between ourselves and our Jewish friends. We regard the prophecy of Ezekiel rather than the teaching of the Talmud as the authoritative description of the future Temple. Differing sources of authority naturally lead to differing opinions on certain matters relating to Israel's future Temple.
4. Richard Ostling, "Time for a New Temple," *Time,* 16 October 1989, 65.
5. Quoted from *Ready to Rebuild,* produced and directed James E. DeYoung (Eugene, Ore.: Harvest House, 1992), videocassette.
6. Ibid.
7. During John's visit in Jerusalem (May 1997) he learned that a team of rabbinical experts confirmed the existence of a red heifer, born in 1996 on a religious kibbutz near Haifa. The animal meets the correct biblical criteria according to the specifications of Numbers 19:2–7. The birth of a red heifer is being hailed by religious Jews as a sign from God that work can soon begin on building the Third Temple in Jerusaslem.
8. Ostling, "Time for a New Temple," 65.
9. Ibid.

5

What Is Next on the Prophetic Calendar?

A historic event took place on September 13, 1993. Leaders of the State of Israel and the Palestine Liberation Organization (PLO) met together on the south lawn of the White House in Washington, D.C., and agreed to make peace. After years of refusing to recognize each other, PLO Chairman Yasser Arafat and the late Israeli Prime Minister Yitzak Rabin signed an agreement and shook hands. It would have been unbelievable had the photograph on the front page of the newspaper not been seen.

In the weeks that followed the signing of the Israeli-PLO accord, two catchy songs became popular all over Jerusalem. They are still being sung today by Orthodox Jews and secular Jews alike. Both songs emphasize the theme of the coming of Messiah. The first is titled "Moshiach" ("Messiah"—Moshe Rosenblum, author) and, translated from Hebrew, repeats these phrases:

I believe totally in the coming of Messiah, despite his slowness.
Despite all that, I wait for him every day if he should come.

The song then repeats these words.

The second song is called "Crack of Dawn" (Yossy Green, author). It describes a dark battlefield where everyone is praying for their lives. Then the night suddenly turns to day. The song concludes with these words:

WAIT! The crack of dawn,
Bright horizon, soon the sunshine,
Yes, Moshiach's on his way,
All the grief, the sorrow slipped away.
The past is but a dream,

In Yerushalayim—the Bais Hamikdosh.[1]
Yes, the fear slipped away,
Like the night so swiftly turned to day.
Celebration! Exaltation!
Young and old dancing everywhere,
We believed it all
Heavens standing tall,
The past is but a dream . . .
Pain so long forgotten—night forever gone,
Now here it is—the Crack of Dawn.

These songs illustrate the fact that there is an infectious messianic fervor in Israel today. In fact, in Jerusalem, there are yellow posters and banners throughout the city announcing in Hebrew, "Prepare for the coming of Messiah."

We, too, believe that the Messiah is coming. He came once, and He is coming again. Jesus is the Messiah, and He has promised to return to this earth as King of Kings and Lord of Lords (John 14:3; cf. Rev. 19:16). Sadly, many who are genuinely looking for a messianic deliverer will be deceived into following an impostor. Yet when our Savior, the true Messiah appears a second time, many in Israel will turn to Him from unbelief. But we are getting ahead of the story.

In this chapter we would like to outline God's prophetic calendar and provide a biblical perspective on future events surrounding the coming Temple.

The Rapture of the Church

Where does the church fit into the events of God's prophetic calendar? Christians have always affirmed that Christ is coming again. There are, however, differing views as to when Christ's return will occur. Some believe that Christ will return for His church before the Seventieth Week of Daniel (the Tribulation). Others hold that the church will be removed to heaven after the Tribulation.

While not all our friends would agree, we are persuaded that Christ will first come for His saints (the Rapture) and then, after the seven-year tribulation judgment, come with His saints and holy angels (the Return) to set up the millennial kingdom. While the return of Christ to this earth (usually referred to as the Second Coming) is heralded by many signs (cf. Matt. 24:4–26), the Rapture is an event that is imminent. That is, it will not be announced and could occur at any moment (1 Thess. 5:2–3; Titus 2:13).

We hold to a pretribulation rapture viewpoint, but we have not embraced this viewpoint out of fear of persecution or suffering. Indeed, Jesus told His disciples that they could expect to be persecuted (John 15:18–25), and that is true for Christians in the church today as well as for those on earth during the Tribulation.

The Tribulation

Following the removal of the Christians from the earth, the world will enter into a period of tribulation. The prophet Jeremiah refers to this period as the "time of Jacob's distress" (Jer. 30:7). Other prophets refer to this period as the Day of the Lord (Joel 1:15). According to Jeremiah, this period of suffering will precede the restoration, healing, and blessing that God has promised His people (Jer. 30:8–24).

Jesus also predicts the coming of a time of tribulation (Matt. 24:9, 29). He describes it as a time of famine, earthquake, persecution, betrayal, hatred, and lawlessness. Jesus goes on to predict the coming of many false prophets and false messiahs during this period when many will be misled by these deceitful and popular leaders.

One of the most helpful biblical passages in understanding the Tribulation is Daniel 9:24–27. The scope of this prophecy covers seventy so-called "weeks" during which God will fulfill all His purposes regarding the nation of Israel. The term *weeks* (literally "sevens") constitutes weeks of years. The prophecy therefore outlines 490 years (seventy times seven) of God's dealings with His people.

The prophecy divides the 490 years into three periods. During the first period (seven weeks or forty-nine years), the walls of Jerusalem would be rebuilt and the city restored to its former state. The second period (434 years) takes us to the coming of "Messiah the Prince"—not His birth but the day of His official presentation to Israel. The first two periods of the prophecy have been fulfilled. Jerusalem was rebuilt and restored under the leadership of Nehemiah. And Jesus, the Messiah, was presented to the nation of Israel at His royal entry into Jerusalem. Christians celebrate this every year as Palm Sunday.

The third section of the prophecy (Dan. 9:27) has yet to be fulfilled and relates to the Seventieth Week—the future tribulation. Verse 27 announces the formation of a covenant at the beginning of the Seventieth Week. The one who makes the covenant is identified by the pronoun *he*.

The antecedent appears in verse 26, "the prince who is to come." This prince is not the Messiah mentioned in verse 25 (Messiah the Prince). The prince of verse 26 is a very wicked person who pretends to be the Messiah. He is sometimes referred to as the Antichrist.

Daniel records that this messianic pretender will establish a covenant for one week—seven years. This covenant will be established with the people of Israel and will guarantee their peace, security, and economic well-being. But in the middle of this seven-year period, the Antichrist will reverse his friendly attitude toward the people of Israel. Verse 27 records that he will put a stop to sacrifice and grain offering. Do not miss this important reference to a future Temple! This verse clearly indicates that by the time the Antichrist becomes active, Israel will have a Temple and will be offering sacrifices (cf. Matt. 24:15). We will come back to that later.

The New Testament predicts that when the Antichrist stops the regular Temple sacrifices, he will take his seat in the Temple, demanding for himself the worship due only to God (2 Thess. 2:4). Daniel refers to this when he announces, "On the wing of abominations will come one who makes desolate" (Dan. 9:27). The Antichrist is the abominable one who desolates and desecrates Israel's future Temple.

The unparalleled desolations of Israel's Seventieth Week will continue until the divinely decreed judgment is poured out on the Antichrist. This judgment will be executed by Jesus Christ, the true Messiah, when He returns at the Second Coming (Zech. 14:3–5; Rev. 19:20–2).

It is important to emphasize that the Temple that will be desecrated by the Antichrist is not necessarily the Temple that is prophesied of and described by Ezekiel. It appears that before the Temple of Ezekiel is established there could be another Temple built in Jerusalem. If this is true, then the next Temple might be thought of as a transitional Temple. Whether of Ezekiel's design or not, the next Temple is sadly destined to be desecrated by the Antichrist just as the Second Temple was desecrated when Antiochus Epiphanes IV ordered a pig to be sacrificed on the sacred altar.

In addition to the Antichrist, there will be many different individuals active during the Tribulation. It may be helpful to introduce the key players during the Tribulation.

The Antichrist

The word *Antichrist* refers to a despicable, wicked person who appears on the world scene at the beginning of the seven-year tribulation. The

Greek term *anti* does not mean "against," as it does in the English, but rather "in place of." This indicates that the Antichrist will seek to take the place of the promised Messiah, claiming the allegiance and worship that Christ alone deserves. This evil person is introduced in Daniel 7:8 as a little horn. In Revelation he is referred to as the beast (Rev. 13:1–10).

His rise to power is the result of his slick political maneuvering. After establishing credibility and trust, he will enact a covenant of peace and protection for the people of Israel. Before long, he will extend his authority into both the economic and religious realms. At the midpoint of the Tribulation, the Antichrist will break his covenant with Israel, turning against those whom he pledged to protect (Dan. 9:27).

During the Tribulation he requires those under his authority to receive a mark on the right hand or forehead. No one is able to buy or sell anything without this mark (Rev. 13:15–16). The Antichrist is noted for his proud boasting and blasphemy. Daniel reports that he will "speak out against the Most High [God]" (Dan. 7:25). The apostle Paul predicts that the Antichrist will take "his seat in the Temple of God, displaying himself as being God" (2 Thess. 2:4). Writing prophetically, Daniel likens this event to the abomination of desolation (Dan. 11:31; cf. Dan 9:27; Matt. 24:15).

During the second half of the Tribulation, the Antichrist will expend his energies making war against God's people, the saints (Rev. 13:7). Although he is at first successful in his wicked purposes, his destruction has already been decreed (Dan. 9:27). The Antichrist will come to his end when Jesus the true Messiah returns in triumph. The Bible predicts that the Antichrist will be judged and condemned to the lake of fire forever (Rev. 19:19–21; 20:10).

The False Prophet

The False Prophet is the name given to a second beast that is introduced in Revelation 13 (cf. Rev. 16:13; 19:20; 20:10). The apostle John indicates that the False Prophet is very much like the Antichrist in terms of nature and character. His chief aim is to promote the worship of his cohort, the Antichrist. To accomplish this, the False Prophet will be empowered to perform deceptive signs (Rev. 13:13–14).

The False Prophet makes two demands on those who live on earth during the Tribulation, whether Jew or Gentile. First, he enforces the worship of the beast's image (Rev. 13:15). The penalty of refusal is death.

Many believers will be martyred for their unwillingness to cooperate with this idolatry. Second, he requires people to receive a mark, identified as the name or the number of the name of the Antichrist. The number, 666, has been the subject of much speculation and will not be fully understood until the fulfillment of these events during the Tribulation.

The False Prophet will share the fate of the Antichrist. Both will be seized by the returning Christ and cast into the lake of fire (Rev. 19:21).

The 144,000

In Revelation 7:1–8 the apostle John describes the sealing of 144,000 Israelites who come to faith during the Tribulation. They are known as bondservants of God and are identified by a seal that is placed on their foreheads. A seal in the biblical period was often used as a mark of ownership, and the seal need not be visible to be real (cf. Eph. 1:13).

The 144,000 are taken from among the twelve tribes of Israel—12,000 from each tribe. The question may be asked, "Who are these 144,000 sealed people of God?" Some would spiritualize the text, arguing that they represent Christians who fulfill God's purposes for Israel. We suggest that the passage be taken literally, recognizing the 144,000 as a Jewish remnant either preserved through the Tribulation and converted at the end or converted at the beginning and witnessing for God through this period. The latter suggestion seems to be supported by the next paragraph (Rev. 7:9–17), which describes a great company of Gentiles who will come to faith during the Tribulation. During the Tribulation, Israel will fulfill its destiny to be a light to the nations, pointing many Gentiles to Christ.

The Two Witnesses

In Revelation 11:3–14, the apostle John describes his vision of two witnesses who are killed at the end of the Tribulation and then translated to heaven. It appears that they will be active during the last half of the Tribulation, inviting a remnant of God's people Israel to turn to Christ.

The two witnesses have supernatural power to protect themselves from the opposition of their enemies—the Antichrist and his followers (Rev. 11:5). The witnesses will be invincible until their work is done. Only then will God allow them to be killed by the Antichrist. Then, for three and one-half days their bodies will be left lying on a street in Jerusalem (Rev. 11:8–9). The rejoicing of the wicked in their deaths will cease abruptly as these two men come to life again and are translated to heaven (Rev. 11:10–12). This startling event will be followed by a tremendous earthquake in Jerusalem that will result in the death of seven thousand people!

The Second Coming

The second coming of Christ was promised by the angels at the time of Jesus' ascension (Acts 1:11). Although Christians differ on many of the finer details of prophecy, we can all join hands in affirming the second coming of Christ.

Isaiah 40:10–11 anticipates that the Messiah will come as a shepherd and a conqueror. He first came as a humble shepherd when He was born in Bethlehem and offered Himself for the sins of the world. His second coming, however, will be much different. At the end of the Tribulation, Messiah Jesus will return to this earth as a conqueror to judge His enemies and establish His kingdom.

Revelation 19:11–21 records John's vision of Christ's coming. He describes Christ coming on a white horse for the purpose of waging holy war against those who oppose Him (cf. Zech. 14:3). He will be accompanied by His holy angels, "the armies which are in heaven" (Rev. 19:14; Mark 8:38), who act as His agents in executing judgment on the wicked (Rev. 15:1; 16:1).

Zechariah predicts that the Messiah will return to the Mount of Olives (Zech. 14:4), from which He ascended (Acts 1:11–12). The Antichrist, and the earthly rulers allied with him, will assemble to make war against the returning Christ. The battle will be brief. The apostle John records that both the Antichrist and the False Prophet will be thrown alive into the lake of fire (Rev. 19:20). Their followers will be killed with the sword of Christ and their bodies will provide a great feast for an assembly of flesh-eating birds (Rev. 19:17–18, 21).

The Thousand-Year Kingdom

With His victory won, Christ will proceed to establish His thousand-year kingdom on earth. This is often referred to as the Millennium, a term taken from the Latin *mille,* meaning "a thousand." The fact that Christ's kingdom will last for a thousand years is evident from Revelation 20:4, 6. During this period, God will fulfill all the promises that He made to His people Israel. They will live in the land of Israel (Gen. 12:7; 13:15; 15:18) and Jesus, descendant of David, will sit on His throne in Jerusalem (2 Sam. 7:16; Luke 1:32–33).

The prophet Isaiah provides some details concerning this future period

(Isa. 2:2–4). Jerusalem will be elevated to a position of prominence among the nations and many people will travel to that place to receive the teachings of the Messiah. From His headquarters in Jerusalem, Jesus will teach God's *torah* (instruction) and judiciously settle any disputes among nations. Since warfare will not be necessary or tolerated, the implements of war (swords and spears) will be fashioned into instruments of peaceful purposes (plowshares and pruning hooks).

During the kingdom of Christ, the curse that fell on creation because of Adam's sin will be suspended and the earth will enjoy a time of physical well-being that has not been experienced since the Garden of Eden. Isaiah predicts that the blind will see, the deaf will hear, the lame will leap, and the dumb shall speak (Isa. 35:5–6). The prophet Joel describes this period in terms of agricultural abundance (Joel 3:18).

During the Millennium, Jerusalem will be the worship center for all nations. Zechariah describes how people will travel to Jerusalem "to seek the LORD of hosts" and to "entreat the favor of the LORD" (Zech. 8:20). They will grasp the garment of a Jew saying, "Let us go with you, for we have heard that God is with you" (Zech. 8:23). And this is where Ezekiel's Temple fits into biblical prophecy. In the future kingdom, the Jewish people will be a light of the nations (Isa. 49:6) as they lead worshipers up to the Jerusalem Temple.

Ezekiel predicts that a great Temple in or near Jerusalem will be the central attraction as people come to worship the Messiah. The Temple is described by Ezekiel in graphic detail—so much so that blueprints can be prepared from his description (Ezek. 40–42). He explains how this Temple will be filled with the glory of God, just as the tabernacle and First Temple were filled with the Shekinah glory (Ezek. 43:1–12).

It is not too much to say that the millennial kingdom of Christ and the celebration of His kingship through worship at the future Temple is the focal point of human history. The lessons and applications for us in this regard are rich and abundant. However, we are getting ahead of ourselves.

Who will be present on earth to enjoy these many blessings of Christ's future kingdom? First of all, Satan will not be! At the beginning of the Millennium, the Devil will be bound and cast into an abyss for a thousand years (Rev. 20:1–3). Who, then, will be present on earth during the kingdom? The apostle John indicates that Christians who are martyred during the Tribulation will be resurrected and enjoy their place in the kingdom (Rev. 20:4). The redeemed Jews and Gentiles who survive the persecution and judgments of the Tribulation will also have their place in the kingdom (Zech. 12:10–13:1; Matt. 25:1–30, 31–46). And finally, the saints of all ages will have their place in Christ's future kingdom (2 Tim. 2:12; cf. Ezek. 47:22).

Postkingdom Events

What follows the thousand-year kingdom of Christ? The book of Revelation describes how Satan will be released from the abyss and be given one final chance to deceive the nations (Rev. 20:7–10). A gathering of unredeemed and wicked people will follow him. But this final revolt against God will quickly come to an end. Fire from heaven will devour his followers, and Satan himself will join the Antichrist and False Prophet in the lake of fire.

Following this, the heavens and earth will be destroyed by fire and thus purged of the damaging effects of sin (2 Pet. 3:10–13). As God's final step in dealing with the sin of humanity, God will raise and judge those who have rejected His Son, the Messiah (Rev. 20:11–15). After being judged before the Great White Throne, they shall be dismissed from God's presence to the lake of fire. The sin-corrupted earth will then be replaced by a new heaven and new earth (Rev. 21:1) and the new Jerusalem shall descend from heaven to this earth (Rev. 21:2). This city, described in detail by the apostle John (Rev. 21:9–22:5), will be the dwelling place of God's people for all eternity.

What a glorious future awaits those who know the Savior!

Endnotes

1. The Hebrew means, "In Jerusalem—the Sanctuary [place of refuge]."

6

Ezekiel's Vision
of the Future Temple

The year was 573 B.C. A quarter of a century had passed since Ezekiel had been taken into captivity. Israel's capital city, Jerusalem, had been lying in ruins for fourteen years. It was enough to make a Judean lose hope. It seemed as though God had judged His people and then forgotten them in Babylon.

What did the future hold for God's people and their beloved Jerusalem? This was a question that must have entered the mind of God's prophet Ezekiel as he lived in Babylon among the exiles located at Tel-abib. Then one day it happened. God gave Ezekiel a prophetic vision in answer to this perplexing question.

Ezekiel 40:2 reports that the prophet was taken "in the visions of God" to the land of Israel. The Lord deposited him there on a high mountain north of Jerusalem. Most geographers would agree that the high mountain must refer to Mount Scopus, the northern extension of the Mount of Olives. However, Ezekiel states in chapter 48 that the Temple will be in an area north of the city. Because of this, the mountain mentioned here may be entirely different.[1]

In his vision, Ezekiel encountered a man with the tools of a surveyor—a line of flax and a measuring rod. Ezekiel was then instructed to give his careful attention to what was going to be revealed. He was commanded, "Declare to the house of Israel all that you see" (Ezek. 40:4). Thus begins one of the most intriguing and controversial prophetic revelations of the Bible. In this chapter we will discover what God revealed to Ezekiel about Israel's future Temple.

Before we get started with Ezekiel's vision, there are a couple of important concepts that will help put our study of the Temple into perspective. First, the Bible is the Word of God and is always, absolutely correct. Jesus affirmed the accuracy of Scripture when He said, "Thy word is truth" (John 17:17). This does not mean that there are no lies in the Bible. There are! Satan told Eve a lie when he said, "You surely shall not die." The Bible accurately records this lie. When we say, "The Bible is always correct," we mean that it records accurately what has or will happen.

Second, when it comes to prophecy, what the Bible reveals is always very specific. Perhaps you have read in Greek history about the city of Delphi where people would go to receive prophetic messages from the prophetess representing the god Apollo. Croesus, king of Lydia, once consulted the oracle to determine the outcome if he were to go to war against Persia. He was assured that he would destroy a mighty empire. Such vague prophecy could come true whatever the outcome of the war. Croesus naturally assumed that the Persians would be destroyed! When he lost the war, it was explained that he had not inquired as to whose empire would be destroyed.[2] Bible prophecy is not like the oracle at Delphi. The prophecies found in the Bible are very specific. There is only one way for such prophecies to realize their fulfillment.

Introductory Details (Ezek. 40:1–4)

Ezekiel begins by providing us with some details concerning the time and place of his vision (Ezek. 40:1–2). It was during the twenty-fifth year of his captivity that he was taken to a high mountain in the land of Israel. To the south, Ezekiel could see "a structure like a city."[3] This is a clear reference to the city of Jerusalem.

In verse 3 Ezekiel describes the measuring instruments that he will use to measure the Temple. The line of flax is a measuring instrument that functioned like a tape measure. It is a long rope with knots tied every cubit. A surveyor could stretch out the flax line and determine an exact distance quickly and conveniently.

The second instrument, a measuring rod, functioned like a long yardstick. It was six cubits long. By repeatedly laying it down, someone could take measurements in what Ezekiel calls rods (or reeds). The attending angel in Ezekiel's vision uses the flax line and reed instrument interchangeably.

The question must be asked, What kind of cubit is being used by Ezekiel? This is a very critical matter. It is complicated by the fact that there was more than one cubit in ancient times. The short cubit is about eighteen inches long. The long cubit, sometimes referred to as the royal cubit or the Babylonian cubit, is twenty-one inches long. Since Ezekiel was writing from Babylon, it seems logical that he would use the Babylonian cubit in making his measurements. This is confirmed by a study of the Temple itself. We conclude that Ezekiel is using the twenty-one-inch cubit that the Babylonians used almost exclusively. Ezekiel's measuring rod (six cubits) is taken to be ten and one-half feet long.

Although Ezekiel was physically in Babylon, he was brought via the vision to the land of Israel and set on a high mountain. From there he viewed the city and the Temple. He was instructed by the Lord to observe and write everything down.

Why did God want Ezekiel to write it all down? The answer to that question can be found in Ezekiel 43:10–12. Ezekiel was to record what he observed so he could present an important message to the Jewish people in the Babylonian captivity.

First, God wanted the people of Israel to hear, study, and understand the words that Ezekiel was going to tell them about the future Temple. This was important because the people were still in a state of shock over the destruction of Jerusalem and the Temple. Although many prophets had forewarned them, the Israelites could not imagine that such a thing would happen. Many in Israel believed that nothing bad would ever happen to the Temple because God had promised that this would be the place in which he would establish His reputation—forever! How could He now destroy this place?

Just as Ezekiel had prophesied, the Temple had been destroyed. But many were now wondering how the prophecies concerning the coming Messiah would be fulfilled without a Temple in Jerusalem. Through Ezekiel God was saying, "My promises will always come about—just the way I promised them. Your present circumstances have nothing to do with My ability to keep a promise." To verify His promise, God provides His people with detailed plans concerning the Messiah's future Temple.

Second, God wanted Ezekiel's description of the future Temple to cause the exiles to be ashamed of their iniquities. The description of the Temple was designed to lead them to repent over their past and determine to honor God in the future.

Third, the presentation of Ezekiel's vision was also intended to help the people understand God's promise about the coming of the Messiah and the establishment of His future kingdom.

Finally, God wanted His people Israel to "observe its whole design and all its statutes, and do them" (Ezek. 43:11). We understand that the words "and do them" refer both to the design and the statutes. God wanted His people to obey the statutes and do the design. The only way in which we can do a design is to build it! Thus, the description of the Temple was not merely for the purpose of information but for transformation. God wanted His people to prepare themselves spiritually for the arrival of the Messiah—and this included building His Temple.

There is practical application for us in Ezekiel 43:10–12. God has given us a similar opportunity as that given to the people of Ezekiel's day. What can we observe and do in anticipation of the Messiah's coming and kingdom? This book gives you the opportunity to study what God has said about the Temple. God wants us to understand the significance of the Temple for the kingdom age, embrace its truth, and prepare ourselves for Messiah's return.

Interpretations of Ezekiel's Temple

Not everyone understands Ezekiel's vision of the Temple in the same way we do. Before beginning our personal study of the Temple, we should recognize that there are at least five different interpretations of this prophecy.

A Memorial of the Precaptivity Temple

Some commentators have suggested that Ezekiel's description of the Temple and altar is a literary memorial to the glorious Temple of Solomon that was destroyed by the Babylonians in 586 B.C. The major objection to this viewpoint is that such a memorial would be unnecessary since the books of Kings and Chronicles provide a very adequate description of Solomon's Temple. In addition, Ezekiel's Temple is quite different from that which was built by Solomon. If it is a literary memorial to Solomon's Temple, the description lacks correspondence in many details.

A Postexilic Temple

Some scholars believe that Ezekiel 40–48 describes the Temple that was to be built by the Jews after they returned from the Babylonian captivity. Accordingly, Ezekiel's vision was to serve as a blueprint for the returning exiles in rebuilding the Temple. The vision would also serve to encourage them to put their hands to the task of rebuilding. But again, there are many differences between Ezekiel's glorious Temple and the one built by the Jews during the restoration. In fact, it would have been physically impossible for the Jews of the restoration to accomplish what is recorded in Ezekiel 40–48. Certain topographical changes are necessary before Ezekiel's Temple can be built in Jerusalem. And finally, there was no return of God's glory to the restoration Temple as there will be with Ezekiel's Temple (Ezek. 43:1–12).

A Depiction of the Heavenly State

Some students of the Bible interpret Ezekiel's vision to refer to the future consummation of the kingdom of God in its heavenly state. They equate the Temple described in Ezekiel 40–48 with the eternal state described by John in Revelation 21–22. However, there are many significant differences that even the most casual reader can observe when comparing these two passages. In addition, Revelation 21:22 indicates that there shall be no Temple in the eternal state.

A Depiction of the Present Church Age

Some theologians interpret Ezekiel's vision spiritually. They understand that the vision symbolizes the Christian church in its origin, development, influence, and consequent completion. However, this introduces unwarranted allegorization and tends to read ideas into the passage rather than drawing out the truth that is there. Furthermore, there is very little that corresponds to the church in Ezekiel's vision.

A Building in the Future Kingdom

In our opinion, there is no reason to depart from the normal (sometimes called literal) interpretation of Scripture when we come to Ezekiel 40–48. When we encounter problems with a literal interpretation, we should seek to resolve the problems rather than quickly abandoning our interpretive approach. Taken literally, Ezekiel 40–48 describes a Temple that will exist during the kingdom (millennial age). Also, Ezekiel is not alone in his prediction regarding a future Temple; other prophets confirm the view that there will be a literal Temple in the future kingdom (Isa. 2:3; 60:13; Jer. 33:18; Joel 3:18; Mic. 4:2; Hag. 2:7–9; Zech. 6:12–15; 14:16, 20–21).

Touring the Outer Court of the Temple

Just as the angel gave Ezekiel a tour of the Temple, let us take a short tour to discover what Ezekiel saw in his vision. As we start, we should remember that Ezekiel was given a vision of a Temple yet to come. This Temple will exist in the messianic age as the center of government when Jesus rules this earth as King of Kings and Lord of Lords.

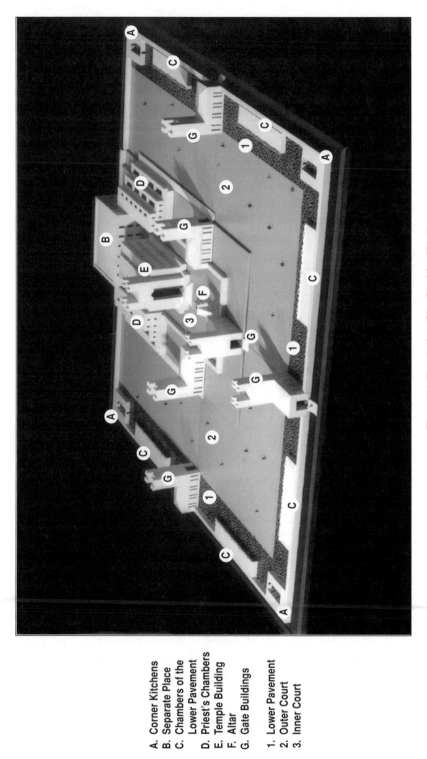

Figure 6.1 Temple Area Plan Site Identification

A. Corner Kitchens
B. Separate Place
C. Chambers of the
   Lower Pavement
D. Priest's Chambers
E. Temple Building
F. Altar
G. Gate Buildings

1. Lower Pavement
2. Outer Court
3. Inner Court

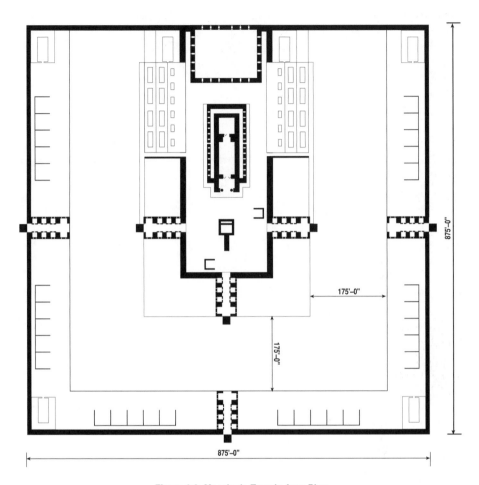

Figure 6.2 Messianic Temple Area Plan

The Wall (Ezek. 40:5)

All of Israel's Temples have been surrounded by walls—rather high walls. Ezekiel begins his descriptions of this Temple by telling of a wall that is one rod high and one rod broad. Remember, the rod is six cubits or ten and one-half feet. The wall encloses the Temple area itself, which measures five hundred cubits by five hundred cubits (875 feet by 875 feet; see fig. 6.2). Nearly three football fields could be set end to end within this enclosure.

The Eastern Gate (Ezek. 40:6–16)

In his vision, Ezekiel is taken by an angel to the eastern gate. This gate is the most significant gate in the Temple since it serves as the basis for

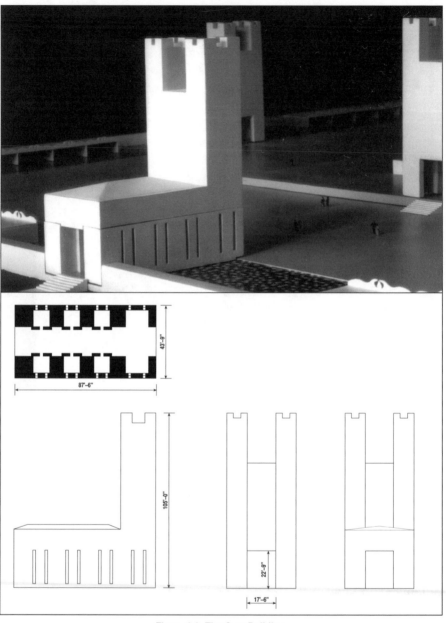

Figure 6.3 The Gate Building

describing all the other gates. Ezekiel and the angel take a very close look at this gate. Throughout the following descriptions of gates in the Temple, Ezekiel refers to the dimensions of this eastern gate (fig. 6.3).

As they approach this gate, the angel measures the threshold of the gate. The thickness of the outer wall of this gate is the same as the thickness of the wall surrounding the Temple—one rod (ten and one-half feet). After passing through the gate, Ezekiel comes to a small room, ten and one-half feet square. He observes that there are six such small rooms (all identical), three on each side of the passageway. Each of these rooms is divided by a wall. Each of the chambers have narrow windows, probably something like the narrow windows in the towers of ancient castles. The entrances to the gate chambers are ornamented with the image of palm trees.

Before stepping out of the gate building and into the outer court, Ezekiel comes to a porch area measuring eight cubits, or fourteen feet long. The entire gate building is nearly forty-four feet wide and about eighty-seven and one-half feet in length.

After he finishes going through the gate building piece by piece, he then measures its entire length as a checking principle. He would know whether the interior of the building was calculated correctly by whether the sum of the measurements through the middle of the building equals the building's total length. It is clear here that the only cubit length that matches with Ezekiel's measurements is the Babylonian cubit of twenty-one inches.

The eastern gate and the other gates in the Temple have towers associated with them. The only detail that Ezekiel provides concerning these towers is their height—sixty cubits, or 105 feet.

It is significant that Ezekiel does not tell us everything we would like to know about the structure and design of the Temple. This must mean that there could be some creativity in the architect's design of the Temple. One thing we know for sure is the floor plan of this building. John's model illustrates the Temple floor plan in keeping with the way Ezekiel has described it.

Outer Court (Ezek. 40:17–27)

Leaving the east gate, Ezekiel begins a walk with the angel around the outer court. Here Ezekiel observes a pavement area on the north, south, and east of the Temple. It is referred to as the lower pavement and is covered with mosaic tile. The term *lower* in the phrase would indicate that it is of a slightly lower elevation than other prominent buildings within the Temple court.

Within the court, Ezekiel observes a number of open chambers that are located along the north, south, and east walls (fig. 6.4). There are ten chambers along each wall, thirty chambers in all. Ezekiel and his host angel

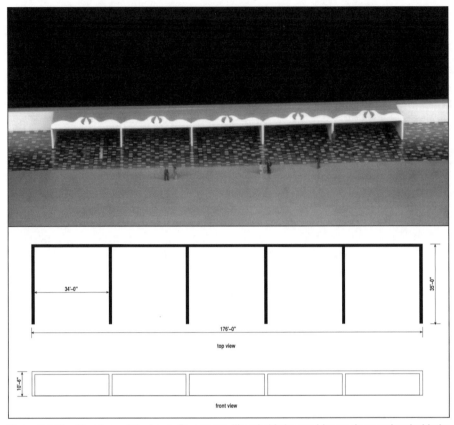

Figure 6.4 The Chambers of the Lower Pavement will probably be used for meals associated with the sacrifices of the people (such as the peace offering).

do not stop to measure these chambers nor do they tell us their exact purpose. We are told, however, in Ezekiel 46:19–24 that in all four corners of the Temple are small courtyards that house kitchens for the preparation of the sacrifices from the people.

We suggest that these chambers are used in connection with Temple sacrifice. Certain sacrifices of the Temple, such as the peace offering, require that the worshiper has a feast, or a meal, with his family and friends as part of the sacrifice ceremony. The kitchens in the corners of the outer court are intended for the preparation of the sacrificial meals. It is probable then that the chambers of the lower pavement are the places where worshipers will gather to eat the sacrificial meal. Ezekiel does not give us measurements for the chambers. In building my (John's) model, I chose the size for these booths in a most unorthodox way. The dormitory cook at Western Seminary told me that a dining room about thirty-four feet by thirty-four feet would be needed to seat a group of thirty to forty people. I chose to make the chambers that size, since in ancient times sacrificial meals were customarily attended by one's extended family, comprising about thirty to forty people.

After describing the lower pavement and thirty chambers, Ezekiel turns his attention to the outer court that is located on three sides of the Temple. All court areas are the same size. They measure 175 feet from the edge of the lower pavement to the beginning of the inner court.

Looking at Blueprints

Have you ever had friends or relatives pull out a set of blueprints to show you the house they are building? Blueprints can be rather boring—especially if you do not have a close relationship with the person who is building the home.

In this chapter we have been looking at blueprints of Messiah's Temple. Although it may seem tedious, these details are important to our Lord. And since believers have a close relationship with Him, these plans are important to us—especially since we will be visiting His Temple!

Endnotes

1. Ezekiel describes extensive physical and geographical changes that will take place in Israel in preparation for the messianic kingdom (Ezek. 47:1–12).
2. Everett Ferguson, *Backgrounds of Early Christianity* (Grand Rapids: Eerdmans, 1987), 168.
3. It is significant to note that from the place at which Ezekiel was standing, the city was to the south. In Ezekiel 48:8, 10, Ezekiel describes the sanctuary or Temple as being in the middle of an area allotted to the priests. But Jerusalem (the city) will be located in an area allotted to the people (Ezek. 48:15–20). It is clear from Ezekiel's description that the Temple and the city of Jerusalem are not in the same allotment areas.

7

Delving Deeper into Ezekiel's Temple

Ezekiel had a vision of Messiah's Temple. Gershon Salomon of the Temple Mount Faithful has a vision for rebuilding the Temple. Standing near the Temple Mount, he said:

> I see the Third Temple, which we will be rebuilding in this place, exactly, very soon, very close to our time. Maybe tomorrow; maybe after one week; but now! And you and I and all this generation will have the great big privilege to come to this place in the original situation, the biblical situation, when the Temple is here. The Temple will become again the center of Israel, a center of the redemption of the people of Israel, and then all the nations from all the world will come and pray, as God says, "My house will be a house of prayer for all nations."[1]

Carl:

When I bought my home in Portland, I visited it several times before making an offer to the owner. On the first visit I looked at the exterior and then focused on such features as the kitchen, bath, and bedrooms. I liked what I saw, but I was not quite ready to buy. Several days later my interest had peaked and I returned for a closer inspection. That is when I looked at the basement, the furnace, the roof, and the plumbing. So far in our study of the Temple, our focus has been on the outer court. Now we are going to delve deeper. Our focus in this chapter will be on the inner court, the Temple building, the altar, and the kitchens.

A Tour of the Inner Court

As Ezekiel concludes his walk through the outer court, he finds himself by the north gate leading to the inner court of Messiah's Temple.

89

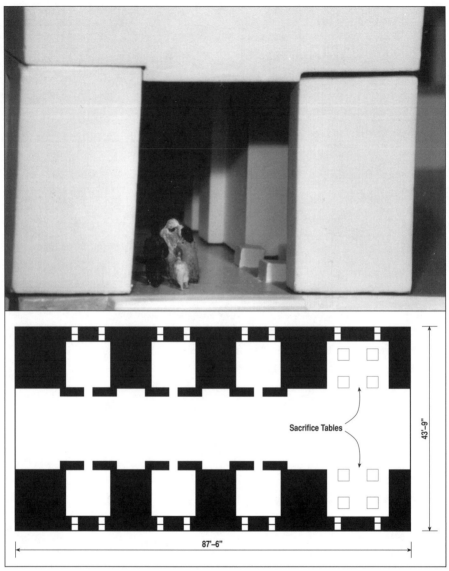

Figure 7.1 North Inner Court Gate

The Inner Court Gates (Ezek. 40:28–43)

As Ezekiel approaches the north gate, he discovers that it, the gate giving access to the inner court, is made precisely like the eastern gate of the outer court. The only difference is that the gate faces the opposite direction. In other words, the inside of the outer court gate is the outside of the inner court gate. This way of building the gates enhances the

The small chambers in the inner court by the eastern gate are for the Keepers of the Altar and personal ministers of the prince (David). These are the sons of Zadok.

symmetry and beauty of the Temple, since all inner court gates follow this reversed pattern.

The entrance of the northern gate to the inner court receives some special treatment by Ezekiel, for it contains some items that do not appear in the other gates. On the porch at the north gate, Ezekiel observes four small tables on each side of the passageway (Ezek. 40:38–41). He notices that there are rings along the sides of the tables. Ezekiel is told by the angel that these tables are for the preparation of the sacrifice (40:42).

We are continually impressed with the amount of detail that Ezekiel gives on the various parts of this Temple, even down to the hooks and rings on these tables. It is obvious that Ezekiel considered such details vitally important and wanted to leave nothing out. We would conclude, since the tables are for sacrifice, that these hooks and rings are places to tie animals while waiting for the sacrifice.

We also learn from this text that the flow of people through this Temple will be in a north-south configuration. Worshipers who enter the north gate will proceed to the exit at the south gate. Those who enter the south gate will exit through the north gate. The eastern gate will be left for use by the prince (Ezek. 44:1–3) and will be open only on holidays for the general public.

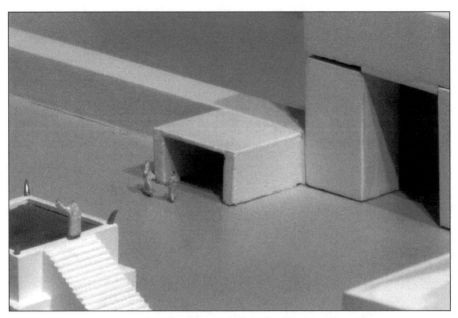

In the inner court, by the North Gate, is a small building called "The Chamber of the Singers."

The Inner Court (Ezek. 40:44–47)

The inner court is an area one hundred cubits square, or 175 feet by 175 feet. Upon entering the inner court, Ezekiel's attention is directed to a small chamber by the north gate and another small chamber by the eastern gate. The exact size of these chambers is not given, but we are told the purpose for which these chambers exist. Ezekiel 40:44 indicates that they are for singers in the inner court. The one by the north gate is for those who keep charge of the Temple, and the one by the east gate is for those who keep charge of the altar. It is also interesting to note that this is the only place where the symmetry of the Temple complex is not carried through. To maintain symmetry, one would expect the chambers to be by the north gate and the south gate. If you were to take the Temple complex and cut it in half and put the north half over the south half, you would discover that the two halves match perfectly, except for one small detail—the small chamber by the east gate. Ezekiel states that the chamber by the east gate is for "the priests who keep charge of the altar" (Ezek. 40:46). They are identified as the sons of Zadok. The name *Zadok* appears quite often in the stories of David, for Zadok was the only priest to maintain faithfulness to David his entire life. The sons of Zadok are privileged to come near to the Lord to minister to Him. In the kingdom age, the descendants of Zadok become the personal ministers to Jesus the Messiah and His prince, the Ruler of

Israel, whom many believe to be King David. A significant application may be made from this. As a reward for his faithfulness, Zadok's descendants are granted the blessed privilege of being ministers to the Messiah.

The Temple Building (Ezek. 40:48–41:26)

On the west side of the inner court stands the Temple building. This is the central structure for which the entire complex exists. This Temple building is similar to all other Temple buildings that Israel has had. It is set on a platform ten and one-half feet high. One approaches the Temple by going up a flight of stairs to the top of this platform. Here one encounters two large bronze pillars. Both Solomon's Temple and Herod's Temple featured such bronze pillars at the entrance. After passing the pillars, one enters a porch or vestibule area before going through large, beautifully carved, bifold doors (see fig. 7.2).

Like the Temple of Solomon (1 Kings 6:4), the future Temple has windows (Ezek. 41:16, 26). These windows are in the porch area and are covered with wooden shutters or some kind of lattice work. The windows are probably for the purpose of providing light in the sanctuary since Messiah's Temple does not have a menorah to provide light as did previous Temples.

Once inside the Temple building, we find ourselves in the Holy Place. It is a room seventy feet long and thirty-five feet wide. The walls are paneled with wood and ornamented with carvings. The carvings alternate from cherub to palm tree all around the room. Each cherub has two faces—a man's face and a young lion's face (Ezek. 41:18–19).

Behind the Holy Place is the Holy of Holies. This room is entered through another door similar to the one entering the Holy Place. Ezekiel does not enter the Holy of Holies, but his angel guide goes in and calls the measurements out to him. It is a room thirty-five feet square.

In comparing this room with Israel's previous Temples, we cannot help but notice that two items are missing. First, there is no mention of a veil. This does not necessarily mean that the veil was missing, but it is unlikely that Ezekiel would omit some reference to it if the veil were there. Second, there is no ark of the covenant. We suggest that these missing items are representations of the Messiah (cf. Rom. 3:25; Heb. 10:20; 1 John 2:2). Since the future Temple will be blessed by the physical presence of the Messiah, there will be no need for such physical representations of His person. We will discuss this further in a later chapter.

Now Ezekiel is taken to the area on the outside portion of the Temple building where he describes a number of side chambers located along the three exterior walls (Ezek. 41:5–11). These chambers are found along

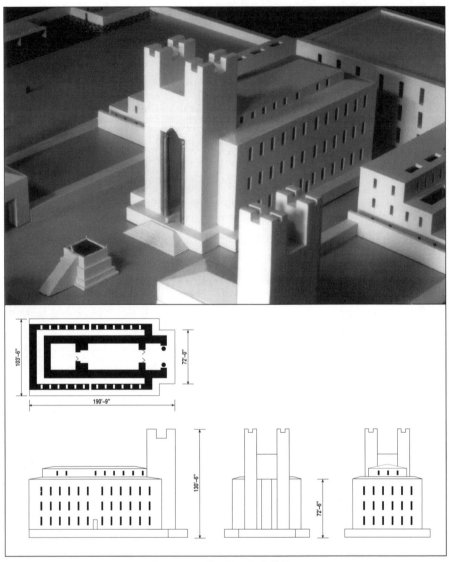

Figure 7.2   The Temple Building

the north, south, and west walls—but not along the east wall since it serves as the entrance to the Temple. These chambers are three stories high. There are thirty chambers on each floor—ninety chambers total. The chambers are entered through doors that are located halfway down the north and south exterior walls of the Temple building. A study of previous Temples indicates that a stairway provides access to the three floors (cf. 1 Kings 6:8). Ezekiel does not reveal the purpose of these side chambers, but they may be intended for storage or could be used for the priests' quarters.

The Temple interior as seen by Ezekiel: a tall wooden table (altar) before a door into the Holy of Holies (Throne Room).

The Holy of Holies as depicted by Ezekiel 43:7, ". . . the place of my throne, and the place of the soles of my feet."

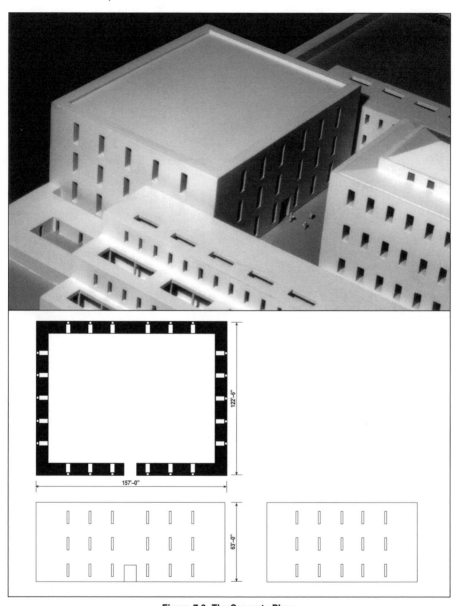

Figure 7.3 The Separate Place

The Separate Place (Ezek. 41:12–15)

In the midst of his description of the Temple, Ezekiel tells us of a building that is separated from the sanctuary and located to the far west side of the Temple area. This building measures 122 ½ feet by 157 feet and has walls that are five feet thick (fig. 7.3).

The question is often asked, "What is the reason for the separate place?"

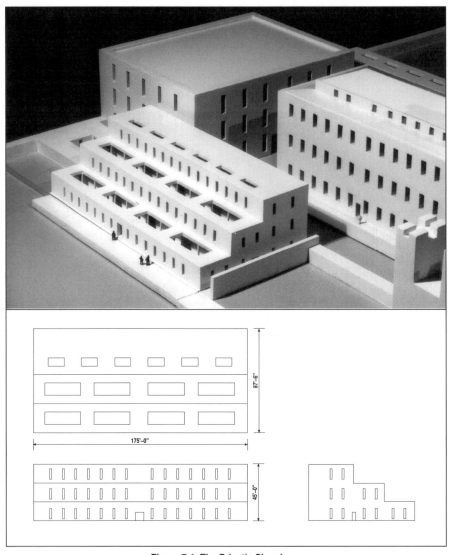

Figure 7.4 The Priest's Chambers

The answer is found in the meaning of the Hebrew word used to describe it. The Hebrew word used here is *gizrah* from the verb *gazar,* "to cut off" or "separate from." We suggest that the separate place is a storage area for those things that have somehow become ritually unclean. Since they have become unholy, they must be separated from those things that are holy. Such items may be later cleansed, restored, or discarded. It is also possible that this building will be used for things that are necessary but not directly involved with worship, such as items for maintenance and administration, thus appropriately giving it the name "separate place."

Priest Chamber Buildings (Ezek. 42:1–14)

Ezekiel is now led out of the Temple building to view two buildings located to the north and south of the Temple and the building of separation. The dimensions of these buildings are identical—175 feet long and 87 ½ feet wide. Verse 6 indicates that these priestly chambers have three stories (fig. 7.4).

The description of the buildings is problematic because of confusion over the meaning of the term *gallery* (Ezek. 42:3, 5). This is the only place in the Bible where this Hebrew word appears. The Hebrew word *a'tiyq* is an architectural term that refers to an offset ledge or terrace. The assumption is that the building must look very similar to a stair-step structure with skylights. Pillars support the open area around the skylights except for the third (top) floor. Because the third floor is the narrowest floor, the span does not need supporting pillars.

The purpose of the priests' chambers is revealed in Ezekiel 42:13–14. These buildings are intended as dining halls for the priests who offer sacrifices and who are required to eat certain portions of the offerings. This follows the pattern of the priests' ministry in the tabernacle (cf. Lev. 6:14–16, 25–26; 7:1–6). These chambers also serve as places for the priests to store their holy garments. After ministering at the altar, they are required to change from their holy, priestly garments before entering into the outer court.

The Altar (Ezek. 43:13–27)

After leaving the inner court of the Temple by the east gate, Ezekiel witnesses an exciting event. The Shekinah glory that had left the Temple prior to Jerusalem's 586 B.C. destruction returns and fills the house of the Lord (Ezek. 43:1–3). After being instructed to describe the Temple to the house of Israel, Ezekiel tells about the altar that he had seen in the inner court.

The altar is similar in shape to the altar in Solomon's Temple, but this one is somewhat smaller. It is set on a square base thirty-one and one-half feet by thirty-one and one-half feet and one and three-quarters feet high. The altar extends upward in three sections, each slightly smaller than the one beneath it. The entire height of the altar is a bit over nineteen feet. Stairs lead to the top of the altar hearth from the east. The altar hearth has four horns, one on each corner. The altar is centrally located in the middle of the inner court, which also places it in the middle of the entire Temple area (fig. 7.5).

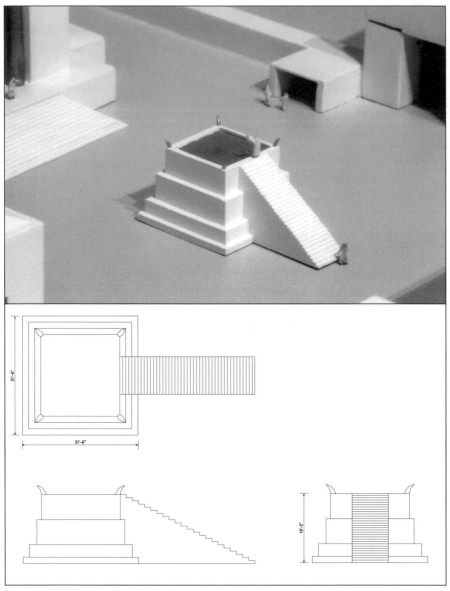

Figure 7.5 The Altar

Ezekiel is told that the altar will be consecrated for seven days by the priests, and then on the eighth day it shall be used for sin offerings, burnt offerings, and peace offerings. The significance of these offerings is hotly debated and will be discussed in a later chapter.

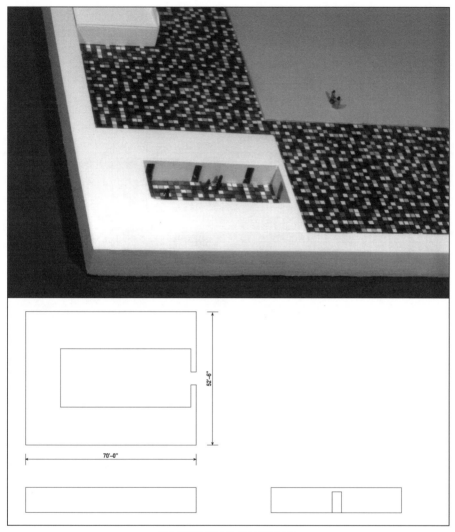

Figure 7.6 The Corner Kitchens

Kitchens (Ezek. 46:19–24)

As an appendix to his description of the observance of millennial holy days (Ezek. 45:18–46:15), Ezekiel describes the kitchens that are used by the priests in preparing the portions of the sacrifices to be eaten. The kitchens used to prepare the priests' portion of the sacrifices are located in the inner court at the extreme rear toward the west (46:19). This suggests that the kitchens are situated near the western border of the Temple complex, on the north and south of the building of separation (46:19–20).

Similar kitchens are situated in courtyards located at the four corners of the outer court (Ezek. 46:21–24). These facilities will be used to boil and prepare the portion of the sacrifices to be eaten by the laypeople.

Reflections On Where We Have Been

Carl:

On occasions when I have been invited into someone's home, I often later reflect on the things I liked about the house. Maybe it was the view, or the stone fireplace in the living room, or the lovely garden. Every so often, I see something in someone else's home that I would like to incorporate into mine.

What do you find particularly appealing about Messiah's future Temple? If you are like me, the greatest appeal is not the physical building but rather the Person who occupies the place. The future Temple will serve as the throne room of the Lord! And He will dwell among His people there. No wonder Jerusalem's name in the millennial kingdom will be *Yahweh Shammah,* "the Lord is there."

John:

We believe that a study of the future Temple is one of the most exciting facets of biblical prophecy. Growing up as a preacher's kid, I remember many of the guest speakers who preached at the churches where my dad pastored. Sometimes they would speak on the issues of prophecy. They seemed particularly interested in prophecies about the Antichrist and the Tribulation. As a boy I felt a twinge of fear go through me as I listened. Most people felt that these prophecies were very exciting. But I did not find persecution and death under the rule of the Antichrist very exciting.

In our study of the Temple we are not focusing on the person and work of the Antichrist. Instead, our focus is on the exciting and glorious future of God's people. Our study of the Temple gives us a glimpse of what we can look forward to as believers in Christ.

Toward the end of the book of Revelation, the apostle John was overwhelmed with all that had been revealed to him about the future. He fell down at the feet of the angel who had given him this prophetic message. The angel responded, "Do not do that; I am a fellow-servant of yours and your brethren who hold the testimony of Jesus; Worship God" (Rev. 22:9). Then the angel added these most significant words, "For the testimony of Jesus is the spirit of prophecy" (Rev. 19:10). This means that the study of prophecy should focus on the person of Jesus.

Over the years I have come to realize that prophecies about the future really do focus on the coming of Jesus the Messiah and His reign on this earth. I am excited about how God has enabled me to use my model-building ability to construct a model of Ezekiel's Temple. But I am even more excited about our Lord's coming and His kingdom rule here on earth! This, then, must be our focus as we study Ezekiel's Temple.

Endnotes

1. *Ready to Rebuild,* produced and directed by James E. DeYoung (Eugene, Ore.: Harvest House, 1994), videocassette.

8

A Temple, but Whose?

John:

It was a beautiful spring day in Jerusalem. Children were playing in the narrow, cobbled streets of the Old City. The air was moist and fresh from the recent rains. It was my second time to visit the land of Israel. During my first visit, I toured the country and visited the traditional holy sites and places of biblical significance. Then I spent a week in Jerusalem contacting Jewish leaders who were dreaming, scheming, and planning for the rebuilding of Israel's Temple.

One year later I was back. I was seated in the office of a busy man—Rabbi Chaim Richman. Before us was a model of Israel's future Temple, which I brought to Jerusalem. His secretary interrupted us several times. There were others wishing a moment of the rabbi's time.

"Sometimes I wish I were two people," he complained.

Many things were on the rabbi's mind. Other appointments would soon take him away, but we had a few moments to ourselves. Our conversation was lively as we discussed together the preparations for Israel's future Temple.

Rabbi Richman raised a rather unusual question. "John," he said, "I find that Christians have almost a morbid view of the Temple. Most of them view it from the standpoint that the Antichrist is coming, and personally, I find the Antichrist to be repulsive. I find it repulsive that you believe he will kill so many people, especially Jews. To know that Christians are excited about a man like this coming is something I find very difficult to accept."

Before I could respond, he added, "Why have you spent so much time researching and building a beautiful model of such a repulsive thing?"

I looked in the rabbi's eyes. After a long pause, I responded.

"I did not build the model of the Temple for the Antichrist. I built the model for the Messiah. The time when this Temple is functioning will not be at one of Israel's lowest points. It will be at the pinnacle of her existence—a time when the Messiah is here. At that time the world will be at peace and 'the earth will be full of the knowledge of the LORD as the waters cover the sea'" (Isa. 11:9).

The rabbi sat quietly. He did not speak for at least a minute. I felt that I should say something to fill the silence, but I could tell he was in deep thought. His eyes seemed to swell with tears.

Little did I realize at the time that I had just quoted one of the rabbi's favorite texts—one that he had recently used to conclude an article that he had written about the future Temple. The rabbi stood to shake my hand and wish me well. Our conversation was finished. We would meet again.

I returned to my hotel with many things on my mind. I could not help feeling a great deal of excitement. What a privilege to have been involved in conversation with a Jewish leader who is planning for the reestablishment of the Jerusalem Temple. The amazing thing to me is that this book is not merely hearsay or speculation about a future Temple. We are considering biblical prophecies that may be in the process of fulfillment.

The Temple and the Antichrist

We do not take lightly the concept of the Antichrist. In fact, the very thought of the Antichrist taking over a place of worship repulses us. However, we cannot deny that this is a very biblical concept.

We have given considerable thought to this issue since John's visit with the rabbi in Jerusalem. Although there are still many questions, the issue is becoming clearer to us now. We would like to share with you what we have been learning.

We must first point out that if the future Temple is to be desecrated by the Antichrist, it would not be the first time for God to allow such a thing. Our God is sovereign. He allows many evil things that ultimately serve to accomplish His holy purposes. This is demonstrated throughout Israel's history. The Babylonians desecrated and destroyed Solomon's Temple. Antiochus Epiphanes desecrated the Second Temple by sacrificing a pig there. In A.D. 70 the Romans looted, burned, and destroyed God's holy Temple in Jerusalem.

In thinking about the future Temple, it is significant, we believe, that Antiochus Epiphanes desecrated but did not ruin the Second Temple. This suggests the possibility that the future Temple may be desecrated by the Antichrist but not totally ruined. Several important Scripture passages relate to the Antichrist and his dealings with a future Temple.

Daniel 9:27

"And he will make a firm covenant with the many for one week, but in the middle of the week he will put a stop to sacrifice and grain offering; and on the wing of abominations will come one who makes desolate, even until a complete destruction, one that is decreed is poured out on the one who makes desolate" (Dan. 9:27).

This passage clearly states that there will be a sacrificial system in operation in the future. You cannot put a stop to something that does not exist.

According to Deuteronomy 12:4–14, there is only one place where God's people are permitted to offer sacrifices. The one place is the Jerusalem Temple. Of course, if there is no Temple, then there can be no sacrifice. Since there is no Jewish Temple, there are no offerings or sacrifices being presented in Jerusalem today.

If Daniel's words about sacrifice and grain offering are to come true, there must first be a Temple constructed in order to provide a suitable place for such sacrifices. This means that a Temple will be built.

Daniel 11:31; 12:11

"And forces from him will arise, desecrate the sanctuary fortress, and do away with the regular sacrifice. And they will set up the abomination of desolation" (Dan. 11:31).

"And from the time that the regular sacrifice is abolished and the abomination of desolation is set up, there will be 1290 days" (Dan 12:11).

Both of these prophetic passages predict the abolishment of regular sacrifice and the setting up of something called the abomination of desolation. Neither of these events can occur apart from the establishment of a future Temple.

Some students of prophecy have felt that these passages have already been fulfilled in the person of Antiochus Epiphanes IV, the Seleucid ruler who sought to hellenize his dominion by encouraging the use of the Greek language and forcing the acceptance of the Greek religion. His attempt to accomplish this goal brought him into direct conflict with the worship of the one true God in Israel.

In an attempt to substitute the worship of Zeus for the worship of the God of Israel, he ordered that a pig be offered on the holy altar, and he set up an idol of Zeus in the Temple. These activities by Antiochus certainly seem to fit what Daniel describes. But we need to look at the second half of our Bible before making a decision.

Matthew 24:14–15

Jesus provides us with a key insight into the fulfillment of Daniel's prophecy regarding the abomination of desolation. This insight is found in Matthew 24:14–15. These verses are found in Jesus' Olivet Discourse (Matt. 24–25), his most lengthy and detailed teaching on prophecy. Jesus said: "And this gospel of the kingdom shall be preached in the whole world for a witness to all the nations, and then the end shall come. Therefore when you see the abomination of desolation which was spoken of through Daniel the prophet, standing in the Holy Place [let the reader understand]" (Matt. 14–15).

Jesus refers to the fact that the abomination of desolation, spoken of by Daniel the prophet, was still to come after His time. Antiochus Epiphanes had already come and gone by the time Jesus spoke. Yet Jesus anticipated a future fulfillment of this prophecy.

Therefore, from Jesus' own mouth we have confirmation that the prophecies of Daniel have not yet been fulfilled. Since the Second Temple was destroyed without these prophecies taking place, we can yet anticipate a fulfillment of them in a future Temple.

2 Thessalonians 2:3–4

We have further confirmation of a future desolation of Jerusalem's Temple in the words of Paul.

"Let no one in any way deceive you, for it will not come unless the apostasy come first, and the man of lawlessness is revealed, the son of destruction, who opposes and exalts himself above every so-called god or object of worship, so that he takes his seat in the temple of God, displaying himself as being God" (2 Thess. 2:3–4).

The Temple and the Messiah

The Antichrist is not the only biblical figure discussed in Scripture who will inhabit a future Temple in Israel. Many biblical texts refer to the Messiah and His involvement with a future Temple.

Jeremiah 3:16–17

"And it shall be in those days when you are multiplied and increased in the land," declares the LORD, "they shall say no more, 'The ark of the covenant of the LORD.' And it shall not come to mind nor shall they remember it, nor shall they miss it, nor shall it be made again. At that time they shall call Jerusalem 'The Throne of the LORD,' and all nations will be gathered to it, to Jerusalem, for the name of the LORD; nor shall they walk anymore after the stubbornness of their evil heart" (Jer. 3:16–17).

In these verses the Lord reveals that in the future, that part of Jerusalem that pertains to the Temple will not feature the ark of the covenant but instead the throne of the Lord. The throne of the Lord refers to the throne of Jesus the Messiah that will be set up in Israel's future Temple.

Ezekiel 43:5–7

In discussions about the Temple by Ezekiel, he lets us know that this future worship center will focus on the Messiah of Israel.

"And the Spirit lifted me up and brought me into the inner court; and behold, the glory of the LORD filled the house. Then I heard one speaking to me from the house, while a man was standing beside me. And He said to me, 'Son of man, this is the place of My throne and the place of the soles of My feet, where I will dwell among the sons of Israel forever. And the house of Israel will not again defile My holy name . . .'" (Ezek. 43:5–7).

The man who stood next to Ezekiel and revealed these things is clearly a supernatural being. Many interpreters take it that this man is Jesus Christ. Since God is spirit and has no physical form, the one speaking to Ezekiel could have reference to Jesus Christ before His incarnation. However, the voice that speaks the words "This is the place of My throne and the place of the soles of My feet" seems to come from within the Temple. This would indicate that the man standing by Ezekiel is an angelic being.

This passage definitely states that a future Temple will serve as the throne of the Lord Jesus, Israel's Messiah. These prophecies must be fulfilled in the messianic age. There is no other time in history in which it could be said that the house of Israel will not again defile God's holy name. Nor is there any other time when God will dwell among His people.

It is clear from this passage that the Temple the prophet Ezekiel presents is the Temple of the Messiah that will be established and functioning in the kingdom age.

Micah 4:1–2

Micah served as a contemporary of the prophet Isaiah. Micah wrote a much shorter book, but it contains some very significant messianic prophecies.

> And it will come about in the last days
> That the mountain of the house of the LORD
> Will be established as the chief of the mountains.
> It will be raised above the hills,
> And the peoples will stream to it.
> And many nations will come and say,
> "Come and let us go up to the mountain of the LORD
> And to the house of the God of Jacob,
> That He may teach us about His ways
> And that we may walk in His paths . . ." (Mic. 4:1–2)

This prophecy comes from a passage that reveals certain conditions regarding the future messianic age (Mic. 4:1–5). The first thing mentioned is that the Temple will be established and that the Lord Himself will teach His people from that place.

Micah goes on to promise that the people of that day will beat their swords into plowshares. God will eliminate all their afflictions, and the Lord will reign from Mount Zion. Much is said in this passage about the messianic age. The first thing to be noted is that the Temple will exist for the Messiah.

None of these prophecies dealing with Messiah can be fulfilled apart from the construction of a Temple.

One Temple or Two?

Biblical prophecy reveals that a Temple will be built in Israel that will be subsequently desecrated by the Antichrist. A Temple will also be built in Israel that will feature the throne of the Messiah. Now we are left with a critical question.

Could these two Temples be one and the same? Or are they entirely different Temples without any physical connection to each other?

Whether the two Temples discussed are one and the same or different is a matter for history to resolve. Since God is the ultimate author of prophecy, we can count on its being fulfilled just as it was spoken. However, some details of prophecy are left unclear and will not be finally and correctly interpreted until the events are fulfilled. At that time all the teachers of prophecy will gather together in heaven and say, "So *that* is how that prophecy was to be fulfilled!"

9

The Temple Altar and Sacrifice

May it be Thy will that the Temple be speedily rebuilt in our days." This petition to God, recited three times a day in Jewish prayers, expresses the hope that Jerusalem's Temple will one day be rebuilt. But some groups in Israel are doing more than praying for the restoration of the Temple. No group is more zealous than the Jerusalem-based Temple Institute. "Our task," states the Institute's spokesman, Zev Golan, "is to advance the cause of the Temple and to prepare for its establishment, not just talk about it."

Time magazine reports that during recent years the Temple Institute has directed the reconstruction of many ritual implements that will be required "when Temple sacrifices are restored."[1] These holy ritual implements, along with trumpets, lyres, and priestly vestments, are displayed in the Temple Institute's museum, located in the Jewish quarter of Old Jerusalem.

In spite of this growing interest among Jewish people for the rebuilding of a Temple, the idea of a future Temple and sacrificial altar has not been well-received among many interpreters of Scripture. In fact, the major objection to a literal (or normal) interpretation of the Temple as described by Ezekiel is the reference to the altar and sacrifice (Ezek. 43:13–27). Does the establishment of a future Temple require the renewal of Temple sacrifices? It seems to many that Ezekiel stands in contradiction with the clear teaching of the New Testament that Christ's sacrifice on the cross completed the work of redemption (Heb. 7:17; 9:12, 25–28). As the writer of Hebrews clearly states, "Now where there is forgiveness of these things, there is no longer any offering for sin" (Heb. 10:18).

The Problem with an Altar and a Sacrifice

The Christian Viewpoint

For many of the world's professing Christians, the concept of an altar and a sacrifice should pose little difficulty. Indeed, for many, a sacrifice takes place on their church altar every Sunday. I am not referring to a syncretistic, quasi-Christian group. I am referring to Catholicism. According to Catholic theology, the Mass constitutes a sacrifice of Jesus Christ on a church altar. Catholics believe that the body of Christ is physically present in the wafer of bread held up by the priest for adoration. And the blood of Jesus continues to flow every time the priest pours a cup of wine at the Mass. Catholic dogma teaches that the Mass constitutes a continuation of the sacrificial and redemptive work begun by Christ.

Martin Luther, and those who followed him, rejected the sacramental views of the Catholic church. Those Reformers declared that Christ's sacrifice at Calvary was sufficient in itself to pay the penalty and provide cleansing from past, present, and future sins. They replaced the church altar with a pulpit and rejected the idea of the sacrifice at Mass. The wine and bread in communion are interpreted as reminders of the person of Christ who is spiritually present among His people.

And so for most Protestants the concept of a future sacrifice is not only repugnant but also reflects an unorthodox theology. From His cross Jesus declared, *tetelestai,* "it is finished" (John 19:30). The work of redemption was completed by His sacrificial work on the cross. For this reason, the writer of Hebrews is able to say, "but He, having offered one sacrifice for sins for all time, sat down at the right hand of God" (Heb. 10:12). Yet, if the work of redemption was accomplished at the cross, why does Ezekiel describe future sacrifices and sin offerings?

The Jewish Viewpoint

For many of our Jewish friends, Ezekiel's references to an altar and sacrifices raise some difficulty. The problem is that for nearly two thousand years the Jewish people have had no Temple, no altar, and no sacrifice. In the year A.D. 70, the new Roman emperor, Vespasian, sent his son Titus and four legions of soldiers to bring the rebellious city of Jerusalem to submission. The Romans set up their main camp west of the city and a secondary camp on the Mount of Olives. After breaking through two outer walls of Jerusalem, the Romans launched an attack on Antonia Fortress and Herod's palace. On August 6, A.D. 70, Temple activities ceased. The Temple was destroyed by fire on August 28. According to the Jewish historian Josephus more than a million Jews perished in the Roman assault on the city. Survivors were taken captive to be sold as slaves and the city of Jerusalem was leveled.

There were two roads out of Jerusalem in A.D. 70. One led to Masada, where a band of Jewish zealots continued their resistance against Rome for three years. When they realized that their capture was imminent, the 960 defenders of the fortress took their own lives rather than be enslaved by the Romans. For these zealots, the destruction of Jerusalem and the Temple meant that they could no longer live as Jewish people. Suicide seemed to be the only alternative.

But there was another way. The other road from Jerusalem led down to the coastal town of Yavneh. This was the city that a Galilean rabbi named Yohanan ben Zakkai entered when he escaped from the Roman siege of Jerusalem around A.D. 68. When the Jerusalem Temple was destroyed in A.D. 70, Yohanan was deep into the study of Scripture, trying to determine how to live as a Jew in a situation where there was no Temple, no altar, and no sacrifice.

In the years that followed, Yohanan ben Zakkai led a movement to modify and update Judaism. A verse that shed light on his way was Hosea 6:6, where God declares, "For I delight in loyalty *[hesed]* rather than sacrifice, and in the knowledge of God rather than burnt offerings." Accordingly, it is believed by many Jews that God no longer desires blood sacrifices for sin but accepts in their place acts of repentance, charity, prayer, and fasting.

Another way of thinking about the problem of sin and the absence of blood sacrifice is reflected in an answer given by Rabbi Rose to a question he was asked on the Day of Atonement. A group of Christian seminary students was visiting a Shabbat service at Temple Beth Israel, a Reform synagogue in Portland, Oregon. This visit happened to coincide with the Day of Atonement, a national day of sacrifice and cleansing for the people of Israel in ancient times.

After the Shabbat service had concluded, Rabbi Rose met with the students and offered to answer questions. After a time, one student raised the ultimate question for Jewish people. "How can you celebrate a Day of Atonement when there is no altar or sacrifice for the sins of the people of Israel?" The rabbi paused. True, there was no altar. True, there was no sacrifice. What was the rabbi's solution to the problem of sin? Rabbi Rose responded with a rhetorical question, "What is sin?"

It was obvious from his question that since he had no solution to the problem of sin, he had done away with the concept of sin. "What is sin?" In the thinking of this rabbi, sin does not exist.

But there is another Jewish answer to the seminary student's question. A folk custom that arose in the Middle Ages is still practiced by ultra-Orthodox Jews on the afternoon before the beginning of the Day of Atonement. According to custom, a chicken is killed and the observant Jew raises the bleeding carcass over his head asking God to accept the death of this animal as atonement for the sins of the family. This practice is not approved by the rabbis but reflects a serious concern for blood sacrifice (cf. Lev. 17:11).

Ezekiel's Altar and Sacrifice (Ezek. 43:13–27)

Ezekiel 43:13–17 describes the most unusual and debated feature of the future Temple—the altar. The altar is described as sitting on a base that is one and three-fourths feet high and thirty-one and one-half feet square. Situated on this base are two similar but smaller platforms. Each is square and slightly smaller than the one below it. The altar itself is twenty-one feet square and seven feet high. The overall height of the base, platforms, and altar is a little over nineteen feet. The altar is located in the middle of the inner court, precisely in the middle of the entire Temple area.

On the top of the altar, at each corner are horns or pointed projections. In ancient times, the horns of the altar helped keep the sacrifice in place. On large altars, the horns were more ceremonial than functional and were regarded as a place of refuge (cf. 1 Kings 2:28).

In verse 15, Ezekiel uses an unusual term to refer to the altar. It is the Hebrew word *ariel*. It is the only place in Scripture where this word is used of the altar. The word literally means "lion of God." One wonders why the altar of sacrifice would be given such a strange name and only in this one place.

Ezekiel concludes his description of the altar in verse 17 noting that the steps of the altar shall face east. This brief statement has caused a good measure of consternation among Jewish interpreters. First, Exodus 20:26 specifically states, "And you shall not go up by steps to My altar, that your nakedness may not be exposed on it." It seems that the altars used by Israel in the worship of God were not to have steps. Therefore, the priests constructed a ramp to approach the high altar for sacrifice. The use of a ramp rather than steps became part of Jewish tradition regarding the Temple altar (Mishnah *Middoth,* 3.4). Ezekiel's reference to steps rather than a ramp have led some Jewish scholars to conclude that he is not a reliable prophet. A second problem associated with Ezekiel's altar is that it must be approached from the east. Traditionally, altars were to be oriented so that the priest would approach from the south.

The problem of the steps on the altar is difficult but is not without a reasonable solution. The prohibition found in Exodus 20:26 arises out of the context of Canaanite cultic worship in which ritual nakedness and sexual rites were prominent. The religious issue behind the prohibition in Exodus is a matter of ritual nakedness in the context of sacrificial worship. The worship of Baal and Asherah involved the worshipers in sacred prostitution.

What the Lord was telling His people in Exodus 20:26 is that sexual activity has no place in Israel's worship. To emphasize this fact, priests were required to wear linen underwear beneath their robes so that the place of sacred worship might not be exposed to their bare flesh (Exod. 28:42). Exodus 20:26 prohibited steps because of God's concern over Israel's possible involvement in Canaanite cultic ritual. But will this be a problem in the messianic age when Ezekiel's Temple is in use? Apparently not.

Hosea 2:17 describes this era as a time when the names of the Baals will no longer be on the lips of God's people. As Zephaniah declares, their lips will be purified from any vestige of Baal worship. We must conclude that Ezekiel's Temple is different from previous Temples in that access to the altar is made by steps rather than a ramp, as stated in rabbinic sources. The reason for the prohibition against steps in ancient times will no longer be applicable in Messiah's kingdom.

The second problem concerns the orientation of the altar. The traditional Jewish altar was on a north-south orientation. This too was culturally determined. The Canaanite people often worshiped "Shamash," the sun, that fiery star that rises in the east and sets in the west. To avoid any implication that the Israelites were worshiping the sun, their altars were oriented in a north-south direction. The orientation of the altar in all of Israel's past Temples required the worshiper to approach from the south. This was traditional rather than required by Scripture.

Ezekiel 43:17 makes it clear that in Israel's future Temple the altar will be approached from the east. During this kingdom era the worship of Shamash, the sun god, will no longer be a temptation. The citizens of the kingdom will be a redeemed people. We suggest that they will approach the altar from the east so that they can face the direction of the Messiah whose throne is in the Temple. Every step up the altar will be an expression of worship toward the only "star" worthy of our worship—the Son of God.

In Ezekiel 43:18–26, the Lord directs Ezekiel in the proper procedures for consecrating the altar for sacrificial service. The altar, along with its four horns, must be sprinkled with blood (v. 18). The altar is to be cleansed with a sin offering and then consecrated by the offering of a bull and a ram (v. 23). This procedure is to be repeated for seven days. At the end of the seven days, the sacrificial ministry shall begin: "'The priests shall offer your burnt offerings on the altar, and your peace offerings; and I will accept you,' declares the LORD GOD" (v. 27).

Could the Sacrifices Be Literal?

Could the sacrifices possibly be literal? Would it undermine the full and final sacrifice of Christ if priests in the millennial kingdom offered animal sacrifices?

To answer these questions we need a brief review of the Old Testament sacrificial system. Leviticus 1–7 records the law of sacrifice and offerings. Five offerings are described in this passage. We will focus on the three that are mentioned by Ezekiel.

The burnt offering (Leviticus 1) was the principal atoning sacrifice for unintentional sins. It was known as the burnt offering (Lev. 1:3) because the carcass was completely consumed upon the altar, except for the hide (Lev. 7:6–8), which the officiating priest kept. The offering could be taken from the herd, the flock, or the fowl. The main requirement was that the animal had to be without defect, emphasizing the demand for perfection before God.

The purpose of the offering was to make atonement (Lev. 1:4) for the worshiper's sins. The Hebrew word for "atonement" refers to the payment of a ransom price. The verbal form is used to refer to the removal of sin or defilement by the payment of a ransom. In the context of Old Testament sacrifice, the life of the animal, symbolized by its shed blood, is exchanged for the life of the worshiper. An innocent life is given in exchange for the guilty. This exchange is symbolized by an identification rite, the laying on of hands (Lev. 1:4). The atonement appeases God's wrath against sin and makes it possible for Him to have fellowship with fallen, sinful people.

The sin offering (Lev. 4:1–5:13) was a provision made for those who sinned through ignorance or who sinned unintentionally (Lev. 4:2). There was no sacrifice available for a sin done knowingly or defiantly (cf. Numbers 15:30–31). In such cases, the death penalty would apply.

The sin offering was mandatory, not voluntary or optional. The name of the offering is based on the Hebrew word *hatta't,* meaning "sin." The offering has to do with sin, but deals primarily with the consequences of sin—disruption of fellowship between God and His people. The burnt offering served to satisfy God's wrath on sin. The sin offering served to cleanse the guilty person from the defilement of sin and made possible the continuing presence of God among His people. Customarily, a person who had offended God would offer both sacrifices (cf. Lev. 16:5).

The peace offering (Lev. 3) is unique in that it is an optional sacrifice. It did not constitute a part of the regular daily offerings in the Temple. The peace offering was taken from the herd or the flock. It could be a bull, a lamb, or a goat. The animal could be male or female, but it had to be without blemish. Before making the sacrifice, the worshiper would identify with the animal by laying on hands. The priest would then sprinkle the blood on the altar and burn the fat and entrails. Then the worshiper and his family would partake in a sacrificial meal (Lev. 7:15–20, 32–34) that would be eaten in or near the Temple court.

The peace offering is distinctive in that it is an offering in which the worshiper is allowed to partake. The offering served as a voluntary expression of thanksgiving or worship (Lev. 7:13,16). This may have been the offering used by Hannah in fulfilling her vow (cf. 1 Sam. 1:11, 24–28).

As Christians, we must consider the sacrifices from a new-covenant perspective. The writer of Hebrews makes it very clear: "For it is impossible for the blood of bulls and goats to take away sins" (Heb. 10:4). The sacrifices and offerings of the old covenant expressed a need for the removal of sin—but this need they could not ultimately accomplish. The psalmist recognized that "sacrifice and meal offering Thou has not desired . . . Burnt offering and sin offering Thou has not required" (Ps. 40:6). So what did God desire? What did He require?

What God desired and required was the perfect sacrifice of His obedient and unblemished Son (cf. Heb. 10:5–10). The sacrifices under the old covenant gave the Israelites an opportunity to express their faith in God and His ultimate provision of "the Lamb of God who takes away the sin of the world" (John 1:29). The old-covenant sacrifices of bulls and goats constituted a token payment that God accepted until a better and final sacrifice could be offered. That sacrifice was made by Jesus, God's promised one, when He shed His blood for our sins on the cross.

It is important to emphasize that there was forgiveness of sin through old-covenant sacrifices. But Christ's blood ultimately paid the penalty that God demanded. In Romans 3:25 Paul explains that God passed over the sins previously committed. God knew that animal sacrifices could not pay the penalty for sin. And when He saw the sacrifices offered as an expression of faith by His people under the old covenant, He said, "That will do for now—until Jesus comes" (cf. Rom. 3:25). The point we are making is this: The old-covenant sacrifices did not pay the penalty for the sins of God's people. These sacrifices pointed ahead to the full and final sacrifice that Jesus would make.

The Purpose of Millennial Sacrifices

If the old-covenant sacrifices pointed ahead to the sacrifice made by Christ, could not the millennial sacrifices look back to commemorate the redemption accomplished at the cross?

We propose that the sacrifices in the kingdom are literal sacrifices that will serve as a continuous memorial that the Messiah has come, His blood has been shed, and atonement has been made for our sins.

This all begins to make sense as we consider the altar described by Ezekiel. He calls the altar *ariel,* "lion of God." Who is "the Lion that is from the tribe of Judah" (cf. Gen. 49:9; Rev. 5:5)? This is none other than Jesus Christ. The altar bears His designation because it represents His sacrifice.

And why is the Temple altar in Ezekiel's vision oriented to the east? The millennial Temple will serve as the throne room of the Messiah. For this reason the altar is approached from the east side so that the priest will be facing Messiah's throne when offering a sacrifice.

The sacrifices offered in Ezekiel's Temple will serve two primary purposes. First, they will remind God's people of what Christ has done. This will be especially meaningful for those with a background in Judaism and who come to recognize that Jesus is the Messiah. The sacrifices will serve as a vivid reminder of His atoning death.

Second, the millennial sacrifices will provide opportunity for worshiping and praising God. Ezekiel 43:27 mentions that peace offerings will be offered in the future Temple. The peace offering involved the worshiper and his family sharing in a sacrificial meal. The priests who serve the Temple will not only officiate in the sacrifice but will also assist in preparing a meal that will be eaten in the Temple court in joyous celebration of Christ's redemptive work. One wonders if such a sacrificial meal might take the place of the communion observance in the kingdom.

If There Is No Sacrifice

Yohanan ben Zakkai led a movement to update Jewish worship so that it could survive without a Temple and without a sacrifice. The existence of Judaism today as one of the world's great religions testifies to the success of his efforts.

Yohanan died in A.D. 80. In his last hours, his disciples found him weeping out loud. They asked him, "Why are you weeping?" He said to them:

> Verily, I go to appear before the King of Kings of Kings, the Holy One, blessed be He, whose anger, if He should be angry with me, is of this world, and the world to come, and whom I cannot appease with words or bribe with money! Moreover I have before me two roads, one to Paradise and one to Gehenna, and I know not whether he will sentence me to Gehenna or admit me to Paradise. Should I not weep?[2]

Yohanan died not knowing whether his chosen pathway would lead him to heaven or hell.

There was another road that led from Jerusalem in the first century. It was the road traveled by a well-known rabbi who was a contemporary of Yohanan. He is known to us as the apostle Paul. As he approached the end of his life, he wrote his student Timothy these words:

> For I am already being poured out as a drink offering, and the time of my departure has come. I have fought the good fight, I have finished the course, I have kept the faith; in the future there is laid up for me the crown of righteousness, which the Lord, the righteous Judge, will award to me on that day; and not only to me, but also to all who have loved His appearing (2 Tim. 4:6–8).

What a difference when you compare these words with the last words of Yohanan ben Zakkai. The acceptance of Jesus' sacrifice makes all the difference in how death was viewed by these two men. It will make all the difference for you too.

If you have not recognized that Jesus died for you, respond to His love and accept His redemptive work—a redemption that was anticipated by the old-covenant sacrifices and will be joyfully commemorated in the kingdom.

Endnotes

1. Richard Ostling, "Time for a New Temple," *Time,* 16 October 1989, 65.
2. Quoted by Jacob Neusner, *First-Century Judaism in Crisis* (Nashville: Abingdon, 1975), 199.

10

The Temple in the Land of Israel

The Israeli people are noted for their strong opinions and willingness to express them. They seem to embrace controversy in both the political and religious spheres. "Shall we give up the Golan Heights or maintain control of that region?" "Shall we dismantle Jewish settlements on the West Bank or maintain them for security reasons?" Debate on such subjects rages not only in the Israeli Kenesset but also in the sidewalk cafes of Tel Aviv.

Even on issues of the Temple Mount, Jewish people have differing views. Take, for example, an incident that occurred recently on Tisha b'Av[1] in Jerusalem. Lamenting the destruction of Israel's past Temples, Gershon Salomon and his Temple Mount Faithful were at the very gate of the Temple Mount seeking access into the Temple area for the purpose of prayer. As they began approaching the Temple Mount, an aged rabbi, surrounded by students wearing black hats and side curls, stood in the distance and shouted rebukes.

This raises a serious question, Why would a rabbi of Israel condemn a religious, observant Jew for the practice of his religion? Why would one religious Jew seek to prevent another from entering the Temple area? It is clear that they have different opinions regarding the issue of Jewish access to the Temple area.

The traditional teaching of Judaism is that it is forbidden for a layperson to present himself at the Holy of Holies. This teaching can be traced back to the time of the setting up of the tabernacle. At that time God instructed the people of Israel that only the high priest was permitted to enter the Most Holy Place. Even the high priest must take certain precautions. Before entering the Most Holy Place of the tabernacle to offer blood on the ark of the covenant, the high priest had to offer a sacrifice for his own sins. If he entered with unconfessed sin, he was in danger of losing his life. The Israelites clearly understood that God was infinitely and powerfully holy and that He tolerated no uncleanness or imperfection in His presence.

And so the aged rabbi did not want Gershon Salomon and his followers to enter the Temple. He was fearful that the would-be visitors might desecrate the religious site by accidentally walking across the Holy of Holies. This makes for a difficult situation. The Temple platform covers an area of about thirty-three acres. The Holy of Holies was thirty feet square. Where on the Temple Mount was this Most Holy Place located?

Possible Locations of the Temple

While there is universal agreement among Jews as to the location of the Temple Mount, no one knows the precise location of the Most Holy Place. Although the Temple was destroyed long ago, the place is still regarded as sacred by Jewish people. It is a sacred place that must not be approached or entered by anyone except for the high priest. Therefore it becomes important to many Jews that the location of the Temple site, and more importantly, the exact location of the Holy of Holies, be determined.

Traditional View

There has been a major disagreement over the years as to the exact location of the Temple on the Temple platform. The most common and traditional view is that the Temple originally stood in the space now occupied by the Dome of the Rock. This view has been well-documented in recent years by archaeologist Leen Ritmeyer and by the head of Israel's Department of Antiquities, Dan Bahat.[2]

Much archaeological evidence has been compiled from ancient Jewish sources and from observations on the Temple Mount itself, which favor this traditional viewpoint. Gershon Salomon, head of the Temple Mount Faithful, has told me (John) that he has no doubt that the Temple once stood on the site of the Dome of the Rock.

Northern View

Other scholars have come to a different conclusion. Dr. Asher Kaufman, retired professor of physics at Hebrew University, has spent much of his life studying this issue. He has written many articles over the years substantiating his view that the Temple originally stood somewhere to the north of the Dome of the Rock.[3]

Nancy Del Grande, a physicist who works for Scientific Research

Institute at Stanford, has developed a new scientific technology that has been used to study the Temple Mount without excavating. Her research seems to substantiate what Dr. Kaufman has proposed. If Kaufman is correct in his view, the Temple was originally located at the site of a small dome north of the Dome of Rock called The Dome of the Tablets. Another Arabic name for this cupola, Dome of the Spirits, also suggests the holiness of the site.

Southern View

Yet another view is held by Tuvia Sagiv, an architect from Tel Aviv, who has done much study on the Temple Mount. He has observed some discrepancies in the two other views that seem to be resolved when the Temple is placed to the south of the Dome of the Rock. His view is not new. British army officer Sir Charles Warren came to the same conclusions.

None of these scholars are seeking to create confusion but all are looking for the truth that will resolve the question, Where did the Temple stand? The biggest problem they face is that the only information available to them is circumstantial, derived from the writings of ancient rabbis and historians. Because the Temple area is in the hands of the Muslim religious leaders, it is impossible to do any archaeological excavation on the Temple Mount. The Muslims do not want anyone tampering with their holy site. This is very frustrating for archaeologists and other students of Scripture. As Tuvia Sagiv told John, "All we want is a chance to look."

The Future Temple Location

Ezekiel provides a great deal of information about the location of the Temple in the messianic community. Scripture indicates that many topographical changes will occur at the beginning of the messianic kingdom. Evidence of this is found in such statements as "every mountain and hill shall be brought low; and the crooked shall become straight" (Luke 3:5; cf. Isa. 40:4), and "the Mount of Olives will be split in its middle from east to west" (Zech. 14:4). Ezekiel anticipates topographical changes as well in preparation for the Messiah's coming and gives us an interesting perspective on the current debate regarding the location of the Temple.

Ezekiel gives us information not only about the Temple itself but also about the boundaries of the land. Thus, by locating all the land boundaries stated by Ezekiel, we should be able to fix the location of the Temple for the messianic age.

Land Boundaries

In Ezekiel 47:13–23 we are introduced to the boundaries of the land of Israel in the messianic kingdom. God reveals that the land of Israel will be divided equally among the twelve tribes for their inheritance (vv. 13–14). This provision is in keeping with what God promised the patriarchs regarding a Promised Land (cf. Gen. 12:1, 7; 13:15; 15:18; 26:4; 28:13; 35:12).

In Ezekiel 47:15 God begins His disclosure of the boundaries of the land of Israel in the messianic kingdom. Not all the place names in these verses are familiar to geographers today. For example, where is the way of Hethlon that Ezekiel names? It appears to be a road. But no one has ever found it. It is probably located somewhere in today's southern Lebanon. Where is Hamath? There are some who claim that Hamath is found in the northern part of Lebanon but that has not yet been confirmed. The Jordan River is not hard to find for the eastern boundary. Damascus and the Dead Sea are easily identified. But the southern boundary has some difficulties. In spite of these questions and uncertainties, we do have adequate information to enable us to sketch out a map of the region and gain some perspective on what the land of Israel will be like in the future.

Ezekiel begins in verse 15 to describe the northern border. Then he proceeds to describe the other borders in a clockwise direction. The northern border begins at an unspecified point on the Great Sea, the Mediterranean. Ralph Alexander suggests that the remainder of the description suggests a point somewhere around the Litanni River.[4] The boundary extends eastward between Damascus on the south and Hamath on the north to the site of Hazar Enan. Verse 18 gives us the eastern boundary, which runs between the Hauran and Damascus districts to the Jordan River. The border then follows the Jordan River south to the Eastern Sea, known to us today as the Dead Sea. The southern border (Ezek. 47:19) extends from Tamar, southwest of the Dead Sea, through Meriboth Kadesh (probably Kadesh-barnea, cf. Num. 20:13, 24; 27:14), to the brook of Egypt (identified by most geographers as present day Wadi el-Arish) and on to the Great Sea, the Mediterranean. Verse 20 gives the western boundary as the "Great Sea," the Mediterranean, extending north to the beginning point somewhere near the mouth of the Litanni River between Tyre and Sidon.

When the messianic kingdom is established, the boundary of the Promised Land will be set according to the prophetic specifications. Unfortunately for us, there is disagreement among scholars as to where

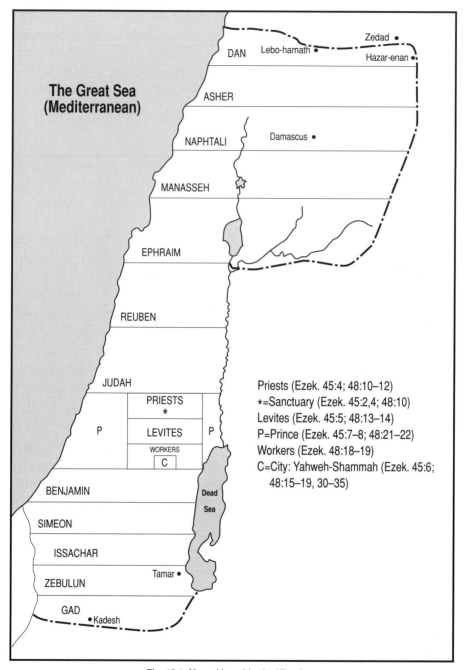

The Great Sea
(Mediterranean)

DAN

Zedad •

Lebo-hamath •

Hazar-enan •

ASHER

NAPHTALI

Damascus •

MANASSEH

EPHRAIM

REUBEN

JUDAH

PRIESTS
*

P

LEVITES

P

WORKERS

C

BENJAMIN

Dead
Sea

SIMEON

ISSACHAR

ZEBULUN

Tamar •

GAD

• Kadesh

Priests (Ezek. 45:4; 48:10–12)
*=Sanctuary (Ezek. 45:2,4; 48:10)
Levites (Ezek. 45:5; 48:13–14)
P=Prince (Ezek. 45:7–8; 48:21–22)
Workers (Ezek. 48:18–19)
C=City: Yahweh-Shammah (Ezek. 45:6;
   48:15–19, 30–35)

Fig. 10.1 Map of Israel in the Kingdom

The allotments and placement of designatd territories are based on Ezekiel 47:13–48:35. Since major topographical changes are expected in preparation for the kingdom (Ezek. 47:1–12), the land area of the allotments can only be estimated.

these boundaries belong. Ezekiel's words seem to be fairly straightforward, but we must also take into account the fact that Scripture indicates changes that will occur in the land. These changes could also affect the boundary locations that Ezekiel gives. Under any circumstances, in that future day when Messiah is reigning, all Scripture will be fulfilled just as God intended it—whether we understood it correctly or not.

Tribe Portions

Ezekiel 48 specifies how the land will be divided among the tribes of Israel during the messianic kingdom. According to Ezekiel, each tribe will receive the same amount of area. There are two tribal regions—a northern section and a southern section. In the center, between the two tribal regions, is an area dedicated to the Lord. It is referred to as the "oblation" or the "allotment." The Hebrew word *teruma* means literally "a contribution or an offering." The word is based on a Hebrew root that means "to be high or exalted." *Teruma* is frequently used of an offering that is presented (i.e., lifted up) before the Lord. The term is used by Ezekiel to designate the center of the land as an offering to the Lord and His Messiah. This area, which is dedicated to the Lord, is the location of the messianic Temple. Ezekiel gives us the dimensions of this area—25,000 by 25,000 (Ezek. 48:9–10). But he never tells us the units of measure. Is the allotment measured in cubits or reeds? If he is referring to cubits (twenty-one inches),[5] then the land area is eight and one-third miles square. If Ezekiel is referring to reeds (ten and one-half feet), then the land area is forty-nine and three-fourths miles square. There is quite a difference in land area depending on which unit of measurement is used.

Some scholars suggest that Ezekiel probably had cubits in mind rather than reeds. It is noted that the previous measurements in chapter 47 were done in cubits (Ezek. 47:3). Using reeds would result in an allotment area that would cover most of present-day Israel from the Mediterranean to the Jordan River.

We suggest a different solution. The clue to solving this problem appears in 42:15–20 where Ezekiel defines an area of land around the Temple called the sanctuary (in Hebrew, *qodesh*). In chapter 42 we are told that this area is five hundred reeds square. In chapter 45, this same area is mentioned in relation to the allotment. Since no other specification is given, it would seem proper that all measurements of this section would be the same. We suggest, then, that the missing unit of measure is reeds rather than cubits.

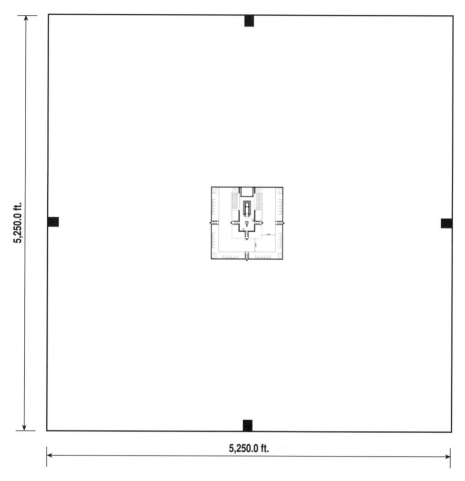

5,250.0 ft.

5,250.0 ft.

Figure 10.2 The Sanctuary

This leaves us with the difficulty of how to fit this portion of the Temple in the present land of Israel. The answer is that Scripture reveals that there will be significant topographical changes in the land of Israel in preparation for the messianic age that will allow for these land areas (cf. Ezek. 47:1–12).

North of the allotment area the tribal portions are divided equally among seven of the tribes. Dan is the furthest north. Then southward are the tribes of Asher, Naphtali, Manasseh, Ephraim, Reuben, and Judah.

To the south of the allotment area there are five tribal portions. These include territories for Benjamin, Simeon, Issachar, Zebulun, and Gad, the southernmost tribe.

Having located the northern and southern boundaries of the land and having determined the portion for each tribe, we now turn to the task of locating the future Temple.

Sacred Allotment (48:9–22; 30–35)

Between the seven northern and five southern tribes is a special area set apart for the Lord and His Messiah. This sacred allotment is divided into four sections. They include the area for the priests, the area of the Levites, the area of all people, and the area for the prince.

The center portion of the allotment is a square that contains three of the four portions. The northernmost portion is the area for the priests, the sons of Zadok (Ezek. 48:10–12). The center of this section is the area designated for the sanctuary or Temple (48:10). The center portion of the area is set aside for the Levites (48:13–14). The southern portion is designated as an area for the people (48:18–19). It contains about one-half the land area designated for the priests and Levites. Within this area lies the city.

To the east and to the west of the square containing the three portions is the fourth section that is given to the prince.

There is a serious difficulty that confronts us with regard to Ezekiel's description of the land in the messianic kingdom. He refers to a sanctuary and also to the city. One would expect the city to refer to Jerusalem. The problem is that the sanctuary (i.e., the Temple) appears to be separate from

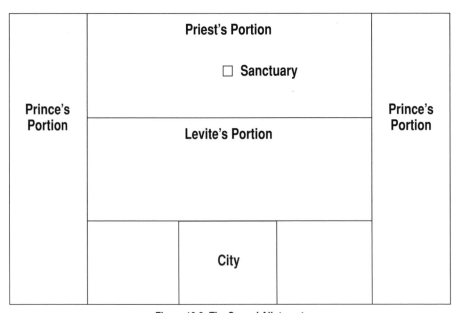

Figure 10.3 The Sacred Allotment

the city. One wonders if the city refers to Jerusalem or some other city. Perhaps a Temple exists within the city of Jerusalem until a new messianic Temple can be built. This question has haunted scholars for centuries. There are many places in prophecy where God equates Jerusalem with the Temple. One such passage is found in Jeremiah 3:16–17, where Jeremiah tells us that Jerusalem will no longer be the place for the ark of the covenant but will be called the throne of the Lord. Some scholars believe that the Temple and its surroundings will be totally engulfed by the city of Jerusalem. At such a time the Temple and Jerusalem will become one. Although the issue is much debated, it is my (John's) view, based on the evidence, that the Temple will stay on the Temple Mount and that the city is a new one built to the south of present-day Jerusalem.

Ezekiel ends his revelation in chapter 48 by disclosing a new name for the future city of Jerusalem. In the past, Jerusalem has been known as Salem, Jebus, Zion, the City of David, and Aelia Capitolina. But in Messiah's Kingdom, Jerusalem will be known in Hebrew as *Yahweh Shammah,* meaning "Yahweh is there." In those days, God will dwell among His people in Jerusalem bringing peace and justice to that troubled place.

Endnotes

1. As explained in the Introduction, "A Temple Mount Without a Temple," Tisha b'Av, "the ninth of [the Jewish month] Av," is a time of mourning for Jewish people remembering the destruction of the First Temple by the Babylonians and the Second Temple by the Romans.

2. See Leen Ritmeyer's articles, "Locating the Original Temple Mount," *Biblical Archaeology Review* (March/April 1992): 26–45; and "The Ark of the Covenant: Where It Stood in Solomon's Temple," *Biblical Archaeology Review* (January/February 1996): 46–72.

3. The most complete presentation of Kaufman's viewpoint is in "Where the Ancient Temple of Jerusalem Stood," *Biblical Archaeology Review* (March/April 1983), 40–59.

4. Ralph Alexander, "Ezekiel" in *The Expositor's Bible Commentary*, vol. 6 (Grand Rapids: Zondervan, 1986), 992.

5. Ezekiel is referring here to royal cubits of twenty-one inches. The standard cubit was eighteen inches.

11

Life in the Messianic Age

Utopia is a word that kindles images of peace, provision, and perfection in society. The word was coined by Sir Thomas More and was used as the title of a book that he published in 1516.[1] The name is taken from two Greek words meaning "not" and "place," that is, "nowhere." In More's book, Utopia refers to an imaginary island where the political and social life were in perfect harmony.

Utopia is a two-volume book. The first volume focuses on the societal problems More observed in sixteenth-century England. In the second volume, a fictitious traveler, Raphael Hythloday,[2] tells More of his visit to the island of Utopia—a place in which the evils of contemporary England are corrected. Hythloday describes Utopia as a society in which kings have been replaced by a republic with strong local representation; every citizen is engaged in farming; citizens enjoy a six-hour work day; family life is strong; the penal code is humanitarian; war is avoided; religion emphasizes the virtues of life; and happiness is the greatest good.

Since the publication of More's Utopia, the name has been taken into the English language as a synonym for the ideal, especially as it relates to government and social conditions. Other writers, such as Francis Bacon and Aldous Huxley, have also sought to describe a utopian society.[3] We find evidence of humanity's longing for a better place all through history.

The prophets of ancient Israel shared in that longing. But they were able to do more than long for a better day. By divine inspiration, the prophets of old were able to look into the future and see the utopian conditions that will characterize the messianic kingdom. In this chapter, we want to take a closer look at some biblical prophecies to discover what life will be like in God's utopia—the messianic age.

The Duration of the Kingdom (Rev. 20:4–6)

Revelation 20 records that following Christ's triumphant return to earth, He will bind Satan and establish His promised kingdom. The binding of Satan (Rev. 20:1–3) means that Satan's power and influence will be nullified for the duration of the kingdom. During this period, righteousness will flourish because Satan will no longer be able to deceive the people of the nations, drawing them into temptation.

Following the binding of Satan, the saints who refused the mark of the beast and were martyred during the seven years of the Tribulation will be resurrected and reign with Christ for a thousand years (Rev. 20:4, 6). The period of a thousand years is mentioned five times in Revelation 20:2–7. Although some scholars have denied that a literal thousand years was intended, there seems to be no basis within the context for moving from a literal to a figurative interpretation of the term *thousand (chilia)*. The thousand-year messianic kingdom comes in fulfillment of the promise that God gave David that he would have a descendant who would sit on his throne and rule the Jewish nation (2 Sam. 7:12–16; Luke 1:32–33).

The thousand years is not the total duration of the kingdom, however. David was promised that his house, throne, and kingdom would be established forever. This suggests that the thousand years is merely the first installment of what will ultimately become an eternal kingdom. The apostle Paul writes of a day when Christ will deliver up the kingdom to God after He has abolished the last enemy, Death (cf. 1 Cor. 15:24–26). At that point, the thousand-year messianic kingdom becomes God's eternal kingdom. After a new heaven and a new earth have been prepared (Rev. 21:1), the saints of all ages will reign with Him forever and ever (Rev. 22:5).

The Subjects in the Kingdom

Who will have a part in Christ's messianic kingdom? Who among the saints of the ages will be there? The Bible reveals that the saints of all ages will be invited to share in the messianic kingdom.

Resurrected Old Testament Saints (Dan. 12:2, 13)

Daniel is representative of the saints of the Old Testament era. At the end of Daniel's prophecy, Michael the archangel informs him that "many of those who sleep in the dust of the ground will awake . . . to everlasting life" (Dan. 12:2). Then Daniel is informed that he will "enter into rest and rise again . . . at the end of the age" (Dan. 12:13). The end of the age refers to this present age—the age of promise—that precedes the age of fulfillment. This is a clear reference to the resurrection of Old Testament saints at the end of this age so that they may enter the messianic kingdom in resurrected, glorified bodies.

Resurrected Tribulation Saints (Rev. 20:4)

The Bible is also very clear that the saints who have died during the Tribulation will be resurrected and enter into the messianic kingdom. In Revelation 20:4 John says, "those who had been beheaded because of the testimony of Jesus . . . who had not worshiped the beast or his image . . . came to life and reigned with Christ for a thousand years." These saints share in what John calls the first resurrection (Rev. 20:6).

Resurrected Church-Age Saints (2 Tim. 2:12; 1 Cor. 6:2)

There is evidence to suggest that the resurrected church-age saints will also have their part in Messiah's kingdom. Paul declares in 2 Timothy 2:12a, "If we endure, we shall also reign with Him." The most likely time for believers to share in Christ's reign would be during the messianic kingdom. First Corinthians 6:2 indicates that this may involve the exercise of some delegated authority: "Or do you not know that the saints will judge the world?"

Redeemed Survivors of the Tribulation (Zech. 12:10–13:1; Matt. 25:1–30, 31–46)

Although the Tribulation will be characterized by death and destruction, many of those who believe will survive. The prophet Zechariah envisions that the Jewish remnant who see Christ at His second coming will recognize Him whom they have pierced and repent of their unbelief. They will be those whom the Lord will take from among the nations and gather them back to their own land (Ezek. 36:24; cf. Matt. 24:31). Not only will a remnant of Jewish people enter the kingdom, but there will be Gentile believers as well. In His description of the judgment on the Gentile nations (Matt. 25:31–46), Jesus explains that the righteous (the sheep) will be told, "Come, you who are blessed of My Father, inherit the kingdom prepared for you from the foundation of the world" (Matt. 25:34).

The Government of the Kingdom

There are many different forms of government in the world. We are most familiar with the democratic form where the people (Greek, *demos*) have a major part in ruling themselves. During the Millennium, government will take the form of a theocracy in which God (Greek, *theos*) rules His subjects through the person of Jesus Christ.

The theocratic rule by King Jesus was promised in 2 Samuel 7:12–16, where God declared that King David would have a son who would sit on his throne and rule the nation of Israel forever. The key elements of this promise are summarized in verse 16: "And your *house* and your *kingdom* shall endure before Me forever; your *throne* shall be established forever" (emphasis added). No doubt for generations the descendants of David wondered, *With whom will this promised be fulfilled?*

The answer to this question was revealed when the angel Gabriel announced to Mary that she was to become the mother of the child Jesus. Gabriel declared, "He will be great, and will be called the Son of the Most High; and the Lord God will give Him the *throne* of His father David; and He will reign over the *house* of Jacob forever, and His *kingdom* will have no end" (Luke 1:32–33, emphasis added). Note that the key words mentioned in the promise of 2 Samuel 7:16 (house, kingdom, and throne) are repeated in the announcement to Mary.

The kingdom rule of Jesus, the divine Messiah, was anticipated long ago in Daniel's vision wherein the Son of Man received from the Ancient of Days "dominion, glory and a kingdom that all the peoples, nations, and men of every language might serve Him" (Dan. 7:13–14). Isaiah the prophet spoke of the Messiah's kingdom rule when he prophesied that "a child will be born to us, a son will be given to us; and the government will rest on His shoulders . . . There will be no end to the increase of His government or of peace, on the throne of David and over his kingdom" (Isa. 9:6–7).

The prophets reveal that Messiah Jesus will rule from Jerusalem (Isa. 2:2–3; Mic. 4:1–2), which will serve both as the capital and the educational center for the kingdom. People from all over the earth will come to Jerusalem to benefit from the Messiah's teaching and His judicial decisions (Isa. 2:3–4).

The Bible reveals a number of significant details about the Messiah's government during the Millennium.[4]

Messiah's government will include many lesser authorities who will share in His rule. The church age saints and resurrected tribulation martyrs will reign with Christ (Rev. 20:4, 6). The Bible teaches that the Old Testament saints will also exercise governmental authority in the kingdom (Isa. 1:26; Dan. 7:27; Zech. 3:7). They will share in the rule of the kingdom, ministering under the authority of Jesus Christ.

Messiah's government will be universal, extending throughout the earth. There will be no part of the earth outside the sovereign dominion of the King (Dan. 7:14; Zech. 14:9).

Messiah's government will be characterized by absolute righteousness and justice. Isaiah predicts, "But with righteousness He will judge the poor, and decide with fairness for the afflicted of the earth" (Isa. 11:4). His judgment will not be based on superficial criteria but upon truth and knowledge (Isa. 11:3).

Messiah's government will be a unified government. Unlike the past, when Israel and Judah were divided and the nations were divided against each other, the messianic kingdom will bring all nations and people together under the King (Ezek. 37:22–24; Zech. 14:9).

Messiah's government will deal swiftly with any outbreak of rebellion or sin. Isaiah predicts that "He will strike the earth with the rod of His mouth, and with the breath of His lips He will slay the wicked" (Isa. 11:4). The apostle John predicts that He will rule the nations with a rod of iron, an emblem of strong and severe justice.

The Conditions Within the Kingdom

What will it be like to live in the messianic kingdom? What kind of lives will the resurrected saints live during the Millennium? Scripture reveals that this will be a period of extraordinary blessing. The prophets provide us with many of the details.

Peace

Because all the nations of the earth will come under the authority of the Messiah, the kingdom will be characterized by international and individual peace. Isaiah 2:4 predicts that people will turn their weapons of war (swords and spears) into implements of agriculture (plowshares and pruning hooks). The prophet identifies the messianic ruler as the Prince of Peace (Isa. 9:6) and announces that "there will be no end to the increase of His government or of peace" (9:7). The peace of Messiah's kingdom will impact all of creation. Even ferocious beasts of the animal kingdom will become gentle (Isa. 11:6–7).

Joy

One of the greatest blessings of the Messiah's kingdom will be the fullness of joy that comes from being in the Lord's presence. Isaiah speaks prophetically to the Lord of how He will bring joy to His people, "Thou shalt increase their gladness; they will be glad in Thy presence as with the gladness of harvest" (Isa. 9:3). Zechariah predicts that the hearts of God's people will be glad "as if from wine . . . their heart will rejoice in the LORD" (Zech. 10:8). Anticipating His resurrection and kingdom fellowship with His disciples, Jesus said, "I will see you again, and your heart will rejoice, and no one takes your joy away from you" (John 16:22).

Holiness

In view of the continuing degeneration of moral standards in today's society, it is encouraging to know that the future kingdom will be a holy place to live. The land, the Temple, the people, even the cooking pots in Jerusalem will be holy to the Lord (Zech. 14:20–21).

Comfort

Isaiah predicts that the Lord will minister to every need of His people so that they will be comforted (Isa. 12:1). Through the prophet Jeremiah He promises, "For I satisfy the weary ones and refresh every one who languishes" (Jer. 31:25). Isaiah promises that when the Messiah comes, He will "comfort all who mourn, . . . giving to them a garland instead of ashes, the oil of gladness instead of mourning" (Isa. 61:2–3).

Healing of Sickness

One of the most thrilling characteristics of the Messiah's kingdom is that deformity, sickness, and even death will be eliminated (Isa. 25:8).[5] Isaiah speaks of how "the eyes of the blind will be opened, and the ears of the deaf will be unstopped. Then the lame will leap like a deer, and the tongue of the dumb will shout for joy" (35:5–6). Just think, there will be no crutches, wheelchair ramps, hearing aids, or seeing-eye dogs in the Messiah's kingdom!

Freedom from Oppression

Today's world is so often dominated by social, religious, and political oppression. Not so in the kingdom! Isaiah predicts that the Messiah will faithfully bring forth justice and establish it on the earth (Isa. 42:3–4). Any violations of justice will be quickly punished (Zech. 14:17–19).

Economic Prosperity

Many of the prophets speak of how the Messiah's kingdom will be characterized by agricultural and economic prosperity (Ezek. 34:27; Amos

9:12; Mic. 4:4). Ezekiel promises that the Lord will send showers of blessing (Ezek. 34:26). He predicts that the Judean wilderness will be watered by a river flowing from Jerusalem and the Dead Sea will produce fish like those from the Mediterranean (Ezek. 47:8–12). Joel speaks of how the "mountains will drip with sweet wine, and the hills will flow with milk" (Joel 3:18)—powerful images of agricultural prosperity.

The Worship in the Kingdom

So far, the description of Messiah's kingdom sounds pretty good. But we have yet to describe the best part—the privilege of joyous worship. What will it be like to worship God in the Millennium? Several distinctive features come to mind.

The Personal Presence of Christ

Through the prophet Zechariah, the Messiah declares to Jerusalem, "Behold I am coming and I will dwell in your midst" (Zech. 2:10). Although Christ resides in heaven today, after His return He will establish His throne on earth (Zeph. 3:15; 14:9). During His kingdom rule, the Savior will be accessible to all those who would like some time with Him. Can you imagine the experience of seeing Jesus for the first time in the kingdom and having the opportunity to walk up to Him and express your appreciation for His dying on the cross for you?

The Universal Knowledge of God

Isaiah predicts that the Messiah's kingdom will be characterized by peace and prosperity because "the earth will be full of the knowledge of the LORD as the waters cover the sea" (Isa. 11:9; cf. Ps. 22:27; Hab. 2:14). The prophet Amos speaks of the nations who are called by God's name (Amos 9:12). The restoration of people to God reverses the alienation that resulted from the Fall.

The Worship Center in Jerusalem

Jerusalem will be not only the capital of the Messiah's kingdom but also the worship center for all the world. Zechariah 8:20–23 predicts that all the nations will worship God in Jerusalem. The prophet declares, "In those days ten men from the nations of every language will grasp the garment of a Jew saying, 'Let us go with you, for we have heard that God is with you.'" In that day, the people of Israel will fulfill their destiny to be a light to the nations (Isa. 49:6).

The Festivals to Be Celebrated

Throughout Israel's history, special festivals have provided the opportunity for God's people to celebrate His person and work. This will be true in the messianic kingdom as well. The Lord announces to Zechariah that occasions for fasting over God's past judgments will become occasions for joy, gladness, and cheerful feasts in the kingdom (Zech. 8:19; cf. Ezek. 44:24; 45:18; 46:15).

One feast that is specifically mentioned is the Feast of Tabernacles. Zechariah predicts that the nations "will go up from year to year to worship the King, the LORD of hosts, and to celebrate the Feast of Booths" (Zech. 14:16).[6] The Feast of Tabernacles is the most joyous of all the Israelite festivals. It marks the end of the harvest season and compares with our traditional Thanksgiving Day. All of God's people will have the opportunity to celebrate this feast with Jesus in Jerusalem during His kingdom reign.

The Sacrifices at the Temple

One major feature of worship during the kingdom will be the offering of sacrifices in the Temple (Ezek. 43:13–27). As we have indicated in chapter 10, these offerings add nothing to the full and final work of Christ on the cross. Rather, they serve to commemorate His work in a profound and visual way.

In addition to the regular sacrifices presented by the priests, Ezekiel speaks of the sacrifices offered by the people (Ezek. 43:24). He also describes the kitchens in the four corners of the outer court of the Temple where the priests will boil the sacrifices of the people (Ezek. 46:21–24). There will then be opportunity for the people to share in a sacrificial meal as an expression of celebration and worship. What a privilege it will be to gather in the outer court of the Temple with Christian friends to celebrate the greatness of our Savior, King Jesus!

Beyond Imagination

In this chapter we have sought to describe what God's future kingdom on earth will be like. We are sure that we have only begun to discover the joys and blessings of Christ's kingdom. In 1 Corinthians 1:9 Paul quotes Isaiah 64:4, saying, "Things which eye has not seen and ear has not heard, and which have not entered the heart of man, all that God has prepared for those who love him."

In my home I (Carl) have a silkscreen work by Sister Corita that says,

"To believe in God is to know that all the rules are fair and that there will be wonderful surprises." As God's people, these surprises will be ours in His kingdom.

Endnotes

1. Not to be confused with the Irish poet Thomas Moore (1779–1852).
2. In Greek the name *Hythloday* means "teller of tales."
3. Francis Bacon, *New Atlantis* (1627); Aldous Huxley, *Brave New World* (1932).
4. For a thorough study of this subject, see J. Dwight Pentecost, "The Government and the Governed in The Millennium," in *Things to Come* (Grand Rapids: Zondervan, 1958), 495–511.
5. Death will be removed except as a penal measure in dealing with sin and rebellion against God (Ps. 2:9; Rev. 19:15).
6. This is no doubt the background of Peter's suggestion in Matthew 17:4 that he make three tabernacles. Seeing Jesus gloriously transfigured and accompanied by Moses and Elijah, Peter correctly concluded that it would be appropriate to celebrate the kingdom feast—the Feast of Tabernacles. He was correct in making this connection but a bit off on the timing.

12

What Is Missing from Messiah's Temple?

Have you ever suddenly discovered that something important to you is missing? Perhaps it was the morning you looked out your living room window and saw that your car was missing from the driveway. Your heart skipped a beat as you tried to think of an explanation. Did you park it somewhere else? Did you leave it at the garage for service? Within a few moments you came to the startling realization that there was no explanation. Your car had been stolen!

No doubt you have had the experience of reaching for your wallet or purse only to find it missing. Where could it be? You quickly begin to rehearse your recent itinerary. "Did I leave it at home or in the car? Did I take it with me when I paid for that item at the store?"

It is always troubling to have something missing—whether a car, a wallet, a book, or a pet. So it has been troubling to many Bible teachers and commentators that there are numerous items missing from the Messiah's Temple! Let us probe the mystery of what is missing from the Messiah's Temple.

What Is Missing?

We have taken an inventory and discovered that eight items are missing from Ezekiel's Temple. In addition, an important item has been subjected to significant changes. Here is what is missing: the wall of partition, the court of the women, the laver, the lampstand, the table of showbread, the altar of incense, the veil, and the ark of the covenant. In addition to these eight missing items, Ezekiel indicates that major changes have been made to the altar of sacrifice, both in its shape and approach.

How can we account for all these differences? This question has been a concern to both Jewish and Christian communities. For centuries, theologians and scholars have pondered the mystery of the missing Temple items.

The Messianic Age

The first key to the mystery of the missing Temple items has to do with the messianic age. This future period will be totally different from anything that this world has yet experienced. According to Daniel 2, the messianic age will be a time of culmination—to bring all things into conformity with the will of God. So it should not surprise us that certain changes will be necessary in order to accomplish this.

The prophet Zechariah writes of some of these changes that will occur in connection with the worship of God in the kingdom. Zechariah 8:19 reveals that days that have been traditionally set apart by the Jews for fasting will be changed to days of feasting. "Thus says the LORD of Hosts, 'The fast of the fourth, the fast of the fifth, the fast of the seventh, and the fast of the tenth months will become joy, gladness, and cheerful feasts for the house of Judah.'"

The messianic age will also result in certain changes in the land of Israel. We find such an example prophesied in Zechariah 14:4, "And in that day His feet will stand on the Mount of Olives, which is in front of Jerusalem on the east; and the Mount of Olives will be split in its middle from east to west by a very large valley." We are also told by Ezekiel that in the messianic age a river flowing from Jerusalem will irrigate the wilderness and revitalize the Dead Sea (Ezek. 47:1–10). Ezekiel predicts that fishermen will spread their nets at En-gedi, on the west shore of the Dead Sea, because of the abundance of fish in those waters. If you have ever seen the salt and minerals encrusted on the Dead Sea shoreline, you realize what a miracle this change will require.

It is clear that there will be changes both in the land and worship during the messianic age. And so the changes in the structure of the Temple should not come as a total surprise. Yet we wonder how to account for these changes. What do they mean?

We would like to share with you an exciting discovery: virtually every one of these changes has something to do with the Messiah and prophetic fulfillment in Jesus. Let us take a look at each of these missing elements and discover the connection.

Eight Missing Articles

The Wall of Partition

The wall of partition was an important feature of Jerusalem's Temple. The wall of partition was a low wall that surrounded the inner court and served to separate the inner and outer courts of the Temple. Josephus tells us that this stone wall was about four and one-half feet high and was of exquisite workmanship (*War* 5.193–94). At each gate, giving access to the inner court, there was a sign written both in Latin and Greek prohibiting Gentiles from entering the area beyond the wall. One of these signs was discovered in 1871 and is now in the Istanbul Archaeological Museum. It reads, "No foreigner may enter within the barricade which surrounds the Temple and enclosure. Anyone who is caught doing so will have himself to blame for his ensuing death."

While the dividing wall prevented Gentiles from gaining access to the inner court of the Temple, the Messiah's work of redemption was clearly intended to extend beyond the people of Israel. Isaiah prophesied that the Messiah was not to minister only to the people of Israel. God said, "I will also make You [the Messiah–Servant] a light of the nations so that My salvation may reach to the end of the earth" (Isa. 49:6; cf. 42:6). Here we see that Messiah will bring spiritual light not only to the Jews but also to Gentiles from other nations. Jesus no doubt had this in mind when He said, "And I have other sheep, which are not of this fold; I must bring them also, and they shall hear My voice; and they shall become one flock with one shepherd" (John 10:16).

Why is there no wall of partition in the Messiah's Temple? Paul tells us clearly that Jesus, through His sacrificial death, made Jewish and Gentile believers into one body and broke down the barrier of the dividing wall (Eph. 2:14).

Court of the Women

The next feature missing from Messiah's Temple is the court of the women. Earlier Temples in Israel's history had two sections within the inner court—the court of Israel, within view of the altar, and the court of the women. These two courts were separated by a wall. In the biblical period, Jewish women were allowed to come into the inner court only as far as the wall. Today at the Western Wall in Jerusalem this ancient tradition is still evidenced by the barrier that separates men and women.

It is significant that the description of Messiah's Temple does not mention a court of the women. In fact, the floor plan of Ezekiel's Temple leaves no room for such a facility. What happened to the court of the women?

The answer is found in Galatians 3:27–28, where Paul writes, "For all of you who were baptized into Christ have clothed yourselves with Christ. There is neither Jew nor Greek, there is neither slave nor free man, there is neither male nor female; for you are all one in Christ Jesus." Paul is emphasizing that in Christ believers become part of a spiritual unity that invalidates superficial, human distinctions. Whether Jew or Greek, slave or free, male or female, all believers share in spiritual equality with the same access into the presence of God.

The Laver

Within the inner court of the Temple we would expect to find the laver, a large bronze basin filled with water. The laver was used by the priests for ceremonial cleansing before they entered the Temple to carry out their priestly service. It is incredible that Ezekiel's description of the Temple makes no reference to this important vessel. Why is this sacred object missing from the Messiah's Temple?

The prophet himself gives us the solution to this mystery in Ezekiel 36:24–27, where God says,

> "For I will take you from the nations, gather you from all the lands, and bring you into your own land. Then I will sprinkle clean water on you, and you will be clean; I will cleanse you from all your filthiness and from all your idols. Moreover, I will give you a new heart and put a new spirit within you; and I will remove the heart of stone from your flesh and give you a heart of flesh. And I will put my Spirit within you and cause you to walk in My statutes, and you will be careful to observe My ordinances."

Because of the washing of regeneration (Titus 3:5), which believers receive through faith in Christ, ceremonial cleansing will be unnecessary when the Messiah returns. The apostle John writes, "If we confess our sins, He is faithful and righteous to forgive us our sins and to cleanse us from all unrighteousness" (1 John 1:9). Jesus instructed His disciples, "You are already clean because of the word which I have spoken unto you" (John 15:3). The laver will not be needed in the Messiah's Temple because the blood of Jesus has provided sufficient spiritual cleansing for all God's people.

The Golden Lampstand

As we move into the Temple building itself, we see more items missing. The tabernacle and previous Temples featured some source of light within the Holy Place so that the priests could see to carry out their official duties. Yet Ezekiel makes no mention of the lampstand or candlesticks.

Why would such an important source of light be missing from Messiah's Temple? Isaiah the prophet spoke of a day when "the people who walk in darkness will see a great light; those who live in a dark land, the light will shine on them" (Isa. 9:2). Matthew saw a fulfillment of this prophecy when Jesus, after his rejection at Nazareth, made his home in Capernaum (Matt. 4:13–16). Isaiah 49:6 speaks of the Messiah as "a light of the nations." John the apostle refers to Jesus as "the light of men" (John 1:4). Jesus declared, "I am the light of the world; he who follows Me shall not walk in the darkness, but shall have the light of life" (John 8:12).

Could it be that the radiance of Christ will make the golden lampstand unnecessary in the future Temple? Ezekiel envisioned the glory of the Lord returning to the Messiah's Temple (Ezek. 43:1–5). Perhaps this vision speaks of Jesus—the light of the nations, the light of the world—as the One who will take the place of the golden lampstand in Israel's future Temple.

The Table of Showbread

Another item mysteriously missing from Messiah's Temple is the table of showbread. This special table was situated in the Holy Place of the Temple and was used to display the showbread that the priests prepared every Sabbath. According to custom, the priests placed twelve loaves of bread on the table—a loaf for each of the tribes of Israel. When the people of Israel ate their daily food, they were to be reminded that God was their provider. The twelve loaves served as a perpetual thank offering to God for His continual provision of sustenance for His people.

In Ezekiel, God speaks of the Messiah's work as a shepherd and provider of His people. "Then I will set over them one shepherd, My servant David, and he will feed them; he will feed them himself and be their shepherd" (Ezek. 34:23). God is revealing that David's greater descendant, the Messiah, will be the one to shepherd and feed His people. He will be their provider and sustainer, thus fulfilling the imagery of the table of showbread.

We are reminded of Jesus' words in John 6:35, "I am the bread of life, he who comes to me shall not hunger, and he who believes in me shall

These furnishings of a typical Temple interior are not mentioned in Ezekiel's descriptions. They include: the Golden Lampstand, the Table of Showbread, Altar of Incense, and the Veil. All are strangely missing.

never thirst." There will be no need of a table of showbread in Messiah's future Temple because Jesus Himself will be there to shepherd and feed His people.

The Altar of Incense

A prominent piece of furniture in Israel's tabernacle and previous Temples was the golden altar of incense. This altar was made of acacia wood and overlaid with gold. It stood in the Holy Place before the veil. But this, too, is strangely missing from Ezekiel's Temple.

The altar of incense had an important ritual purpose in Israel's sacrificial system. It was there that incense burned in the morning and evening at the time of prayer. The incense ascending from the altar served to illustrate that the prayers of His people were something like a sweet perfume to God. The burning incense also depicts the intercessory work of our Lord Jesus Christ (Heb. 7:25). But we discover in our study of Ezekiel that there is no altar of incense in Messiah's Temple. Does this mean that there will be no sweet savor of prayer in the messianic kingdom?

The prophet Zechariah seems to believe otherwise. He writes in Zechariah 8:20–21, "Thus says the LORD of Hosts, 'It will yet be that peoples will come, even the inhabitants of many cities; and the inhabitants of one will go to another saying, "Let us go at once to entreat the favor of the LORD, and to seek the LORD of hosts."'" Verse 23 adds, "Thus says the LORD of hosts, 'In those days, ten men from the nations will grasp the garment of a Jew saying, 'Let us go with you, for we have heard that God is with you.'" Ezekiel makes it clear in the last words of his prophecy that God will be present in Jerusalem during the messianic kingdom. He tells us that "the name of the city from that day shall be 'The LORD is there [*Yahweh Shammah*]'" (Ezek. 48:35).

During the messianic kingdom there will be no need for the altar of incense in the Temple because the Messiah Himself will be present in Jerusalem and available to hear the petitions of His people. In Ezekiel's future Temple, Jesus Himself takes the place of the altar of incense.

The Veil

One of the most intriguing items missing from the Temple is the veil. The veil, made of fine linen and ornamented with cherubim, served as a partition between the Holy Place and the Most Holy Place. Ezekiel refers only to a doorway into the Holy of Holies and makes no comment about a veil (Ezek. 41:3–4, 21–25). The prophet provides us with many details regarding the Temple, including the doors, the number of panels on each door, and the carvings on each of the panels. Obviously, he is not being vague and overlooking items. The omission of any reference to the veil is not because Ezekiel is negligent in giving a complete description. He is being very careful to give all the necessary details. Ezekiel's careful adherence to detail is why the omission of any reference to the veil seems so very significant.

Scripture records that when Jesus died on the cross the Temple veil was torn in half—from top to bottom. When a person receives a new credit card, he or she is told to destroy the old credit card by cutting it in half. This is precisely what God did with the veil when Jesus put an end to the old covenant by His sacrificial death. God destroyed the veil of the Temple to symbolize the end of the old covenant and the inauguration of a new way of access to God through faith in His Son. The prophet Isaiah may allude to the removal of the Temple veil when he writes, "And on this mountain He will swallow up the covering which is over all peoples, even the veil which is stretched over all nations" (25:7). There is no veil in the Messiah's Temple because our Savior will be present in Jerusalem. Jesus Himself has fulfilled the prophetic significance of the Temple veil.

The Ark of the Covenant

There is one more item that Ezekiel does not include in his description of the future Temple. It is the ark of the covenant. The ark was about the size of a small desk. On the top of the ark was the mercy seat, or the place of propitiation, where sacrificial blood was offered. The ark of the covenant always served as a sign of God's presence among His people Israel. The Lord told Moses, "I will meet with you, and from above the mercy seat, from between the two cherubim which are upon the ark of the testimony, I will speak to you" (Exod. 25:22). When the Israelites were wandering in the wilderness, the ark always led the way. When Israel entered the land of Canaan, the priests held the ark in the middle of the Jordan while the people crossed. On occasion the ark was taken by the Israelites into battle as a reminder that God was with them. Even when the ark was captured by the Philistines, their god, Dagon, fell down before the ark as if to pay respects to the God it represented.

If the future Temple represents the presence of God among His people, why would Ezekiel leave out an item that clearly represents God? Jeremiah has some interesting thoughts to help us understand this

The ark of the covenant has a most interesting history. It was part of the Tabernacle and Solomon's Temple, missing during the Second Temple period, and also absent in Ezekiel's Temple.

mystery. He writes, "'Behold the days are coming,' declares the Lord, 'when I shall raise up for David a righteous Branch; and He will reign as king and act wisely and do justice and righteousness in the land. In His days Judah will be saved and Israel will dwell securely; and this is His name by which he shall be called, the Lord of our righteousness'" (Jer. 23:5–6).

Jeremiah tells us that the coming Messiah will not only be a "branch" of David but also will be "the Lord our Righteousness," the very One whom the ark of the covenant represents.

Further clarification is seen in Jeremiah 3:16–17,

> "And it shall be in those days when you are multiplied and increased in the land," declares the Lord, "they shall say no more, 'The ark of the covenant of the Lord.' And it shall not come to mind nor shall they remember it, nor shall they miss it, nor shall it be made again. At that time they shall call Jerusalem 'The throne of the Lord,' and all the nations will be gathered to it, to Jerusalem, for the name of the Lord . . ."

Here we see that the ark of the covenant is missing from Messiah's Temple to make room for the throne of the Lord. Ezekiel himself confirms the fact that the throne of the Lord is present in this Temple. He writes,

> "And the Spirit lifted me up and brought me into the inner court; and behold the glory of the Lord filled the house. Then I heard one speaking to me from the house, while a man was standing beside me. And He said to me, 'Son of man, this is the place of My throne and the place of the soles of My feet, where I will dwell among the sons of Israel forever . . .'" (Ezek. 43:5–7).

The reason that the ark of the covenant is missing from the future Temple is because the throne of the Lord is present. The Lord Jesus, the Righteous One, shall sit upon His throne as King Messiah in Ezekiel's Temple.

An Altered Altar

Not only are there eight items missing from Messiah's Temple, but another extremely significant change occurs in Messiah's future Temple. This change has to do with the altar of sacrifice that stood in the inner court. Every previous altar in Israel's Temple history was approached from the south, apparently by a ramp. Yet Ezekiel specifically states that the steps of the altar shall face the east (Ezek. 43:17). The direction and means by which one approaches the altar has been changed! Instead of using a ramp from the south, the altar in the future Temple will be approached by steps from the east.

It is significant that the ancient scholars and translators regarded Ezekiel's words to be correct, as reflected in the Septuagint's translation of this verse. The Hebrew word for "steps" was clearly understood to mean steps.

There is a significant reason why the Israelites were never allowed to approach the altar of sacrifice from the east. The pagans approached their altars from the east to worship the sun. God wanted a clear distinction between pagan worship and the worship that He accepted from His people.

During the messianic kingdom, many things will be different. Idolatry will not be a problem as it was for ancient Israel. Furthermore, since the Lord Himself will have His throne in the Temple, it will be most appropriate for those officiating at the altar to be facing the Lord in the Temple. Those offering a sacrifice will approach the altar from the east side, moving in the direction of the Lord who will be sitting in His Temple on His throne.

Another intriguing feature about this sacrificial altar is in the word used to describe it. The Hebrew word *mizbach* is the word that is used to refer to the altar in every Scripture passage except for one. The one exception is found in Ezekiel 43:15–16, a passage that describes the altar in Messiah's Temple. Here the word used to refer to the altar is the Hebrew *ariel*. If *ariel* were a common synonym for *mizbach*, there would be little reason to pursue this matter. However, the fact that *ariel* is used only here suggests that the change in terminology must be significant.

The key to this mystery is in the root meaning of the word *ariel*. The Hebrew root means "lion of God." Remember Jacob's blessing on his son Judah shortly before his death. Jacob said, "Judah is a lion's whelp . . . he crouches, he lies down as a lion" (Gen. 49:9). Then Jacob adds, "The scepter shall not depart from Judah, nor the ruler's staff from between his feet until Shiloh comes" (Gen. 49:10). These verses refer to the fact that the Messiah will be a descendant of Judah. Later, in Revelation 5:5, Jesus is referred to as "the Lion that is from the tribe of Judah."

John the Baptist introduced Jesus as the Lamb of God (John 1:29). But when He comes to establish His kingdom, He will be as the Lion of Judah. So it is apropos that the altar in Ezekiel's Temple is named *Ariel* (lion of God) in Messiah's honor.

Precedents for Change

Is it reasonable to assume that God will make all of these changes when establishing His future Temple? As we have seen, many changes will take place during the transition into the messianic age. God has often changed the methods that He used to reveal Himself and accomplish His purposes. Daniel acknowledged this when he answered King Nebuchadnezzar with the words, "Let the name of God be blessed forever and ever, for wisdom and power belong to Him and it is He who changes the times and the epochs" (Dan. 2:20–21).

God changed many things after the world flood in the time of Noah. He changed many things for Israel as they moved from the wilderness to occupy the Promised Land. And God changed many things when Jesus died on the cross. Therefore, it is reasonable to expect that God will again change many things when He comes into His kingdom on earth.

There is, however, something that will never change. God's character will remain the same forever and ever. This is clear from Malachi 3:6, "For I, the LORD, do not change."

13

Preparing for Your Future

As we have seen throughout this book, a study of Ezekiel's Temple is just one dimension of the exciting subject of biblical prophecy. What are the implications of this study for our lives as Christians? Should the study of prophecy make a difference? Dr. John Walvoord, former president of Dallas Theological Seminary, might well be considered the "dean" of Bible prophecy. He has been teaching and preaching on this exciting subject for more than fifty years. In an interview regarding his book *Armageddon, Oil and the Middle East Crisis,* Walvoord was asked where Operation Desert Storm fit into biblical prophecy. He responded, "I do not think the Bible speaks about this war or talks about Saddam Hussein." Instead, he suggests the current events often interpreted by popular speakers as the fulfillment of prophecy are merely the preliminaries.

Many details of prophecy are subject to a variety of interpretations. One needs to be careful to avoid undo speculation on nonessential details. Walvoord offers this perspective: "I believe Christ is coming and the bottom line in life is how you meet Him. All these other details are immaterial."[1]

First Things First

Does Christ have His proper place in your life? In the Berlin Art Gallery, there hangs a painting by the great German painter Adolf Menzel (1815–1905). The painting is intended to portray Frederick the Great speaking with some of his generals. But the painting is only partially finished. Menzel carefully painted all the background and the generals, but he left the king until last. While he was able to sketch the outline of Frederick the Great in charcoal, Menzel died before he was able to finish the painting in oil.

Like Menzel, many people spend their lives giving attention to areas of relative insignificance and leave out Christ—the King—until last. Some people come to the end of their earthly existence without having put Christ into His proper place in their lives. Do not let that happen to you. If you have not accepted Jesus Christ as your personal Lord and Savior, acknowledge that He died for you. By faith, receive His forgiveness of your sins and the gift of eternal life.

The story is told of a police officer who was patroling a neighborhood when he heard the sound of a crying child. Turning around, he saw a little boy sitting on the curb. "I'm lost," said the child. "Please take me home."

The police officer tried to discover where the boy lived. He named streets, shops, and hotels to jog the child's memory. Then he remembered the church in the center of town with a large white cross towering over the landscape. He pointed to the cross and asked, "Do you live anywhere near that?" The boy's face brightened. "Yes," he said. "Take me to the cross. I can find my way home from there."

If you are wandering in darkness and wondering what life is all about, come to the cross of Jesus. You will find your way home from there.

Making a Difference in Life

A proper understanding of biblical prophecy will make a difference in your life. It is significant, we believe, that every time we have a reference in Scripture to the blessed hope (Titus 2:13) of the Lord's return, we find some mention of how this doctrine applies to life.

An Encouraging Hope (John 14:1–3)

When the disciples were told by Jesus that He was going away (John 13:33), a look of despair must have appeared on their faces. Jesus immediately dealt with this discouragement by announcing the purpose of His departure. Jesus' departure from this earth would secure access to heaven for His followers (John 14:1–2). He was leaving earth to prepare a heavenly home for His disciples. With the announcement of His departure, Jesus also promises His return. "And if I go and prepare a place for you, I will come again, and receive you to Myself; that where I am, there you may be also" (John 14:3).

If you are a discouraged believer, the promise of Christ's return can make a difference. There is something better coming. And it could be just around the corner.

A Comforting Hope (1 Thess. 4:13–18)

The believers at Thessalonica were upset. They mistakenly thought that those who died before the Rapture would miss out on it. They concluded that the Rapture was for the living saints only. In 1 Thessalonians 4:13–18

Paul writes to clarify the relationship between the living and the dead at the time of the Rapture. The point of the passage is that those who are dead in Christ will be raised first, and then the living saints will follow. Paul assures his readers that the dead in Christ will not miss out on the glorious reign of Christ.

This is comforting news to those who have lost loved ones. Paul writes, "Therefore comfort one another with these words" (1 Thess. 4:18). It is wonderful to know that on the day that Jesus comes for His church, those who have died in Christ will be raised. And we will be with them and with Christ forever.

A Motivating Hope (1 Cor. 15:50–58)

The church at Corinth was involved in a controversy over the issue of the Resurrection. In dealing with this problem, Paul first establishes the fact of Christ's resurrection. Then, he argues, the unity between Christ and the believers suggests that His resurrection must result in ours.

For many, the resurrection body will be obtained through death. But what about those who are alive at the Lord's coming? Paul explains that those who are alive at Christ's coming will be suddenly changed and given glorified bodies (1 Cor. 15:51–53). For Paul, this discussion is not merely academic. It has very practical implications. In the last verse of the chapter, Paul points out that the anticipation of Christ's return is a motivation for Christian service. "Therefore, my beloved brethren, be steadfast, immovable, always abounding in the work of the Lord, knowing that your toil is not in vain in the Lord" (1 Cor. 15:58).

No one knows how long we have before the Lord's coming. As Christians, we want to make each day count for eternity.

A Purifying Hope (1 John 3:1–2)

In 1 John 3, the apostle John argues that the believer's conduct ought to be in conformity with his or her confession. In verses 2–3, he provides a key motivation for proper Christian conduct. "And everyone who has this hope fixed on Him purifies himself, just as He is pure" (1 John 3:3). The prospect of meeting Christ at the time of His return serves as an incentive to personal purity. None of us would want to be found in a compromising situation at the Lord's return for His church. None of us would want to meet the Lord with lives that are soiled by the evil of this world.

Come, Lord Jesus

At the end of His revelation, the Lord Jesus spoke to the apostle John and announced, "Yes, I am coming quickly" (Rev. 22:20). John responded with the words, "Amen. Come, Lord Jesus." And so we respond as believers to the promise of Christ's coming. He is coming again to judge His enemies, defeat Satan, take His rightful throne, and rule His kingdom. His coming is closer now than when it was announced to John. We do not know if it will be today, tomorrow, or next year. But He is coming.

Until He comes, may the anticipation of His coming make a difference in our lives. May the thoughts of His return encourage us when we face troubled times, comfort us over the loss of Christian loved ones, motivate us for serving Christ's church, and turn us from impurity when temptations arise.

In a city near Edinburgh, Scotland, a fishing fleet goes out each year on a long fishing expedition. At the first sight of the fleet's return, the whole town assembles on the docks to watch and wait for the arrival of loved ones. The fishermen have been at sea for several weeks, and family members are anxious to be reunited.

During one such return, the captain stood on the deck of the ship with his field glasses calling out the names of the fishermen's families in the distance.

"Bill, I see your wife and son on the dock. John, your wife and children are there."

Each fisherman was relieved to know that all was well and that their families awaited their arrival. Then one man asked, "Do you see my wife, captain?"

"No, Michael. She's not there."

Michael began to worry about his wife. Why was she not watching for him at the dock?

When the ship arrived at the dock, the men greeted their families. But Michael hurried up to his cottage on the hill. As he stepped through the front door, there was his wife in the kitchen.

"Oh, Michael," she exclaimed. "I have been waiting for you."

Michael replied, "The wives of the other men were *watching* for them."

As believers in the Lord Jesus, we are awaiting the Lord's return. But let us also be watching with expectancy.

Thoughts from the Mount of Olives

John:

During my last visit to Jerusalem, I spent the better part of an afternoon overlooking the Old City of Jerusalem from the Mount of Olives.

Someone once said that the most important events that have taken place in the history of the world could have been viewed from the Mount of Olives—the offering of Isaac, the building of Solomon's Temple, the crucifixion of our Savior, the ascension of Jesus. And, according to Zechariah 14:4, the most important future event—the Second Coming—will be viewed from Olivet too!

As I stood there on the summit of the Mount of Olives, I looked across the Kidron Valley to the eastern gate of Jerusalem and beyond that to the Temple Mount where the Dome of the Rock stands today.

Someday, I thought to myself, *it will all be different. There on the Temple Mount will stand the Messiah's Temple—the place of the Messiah's throne. And from that place, King Jesus will rule and reign over all the earth.*

It almost seems like a dream. However, it is a dream that will come true. One day, Messiah's Temple will be more than pictures, diagrams, and a model. It will be a functioning reality.

In *The Last Battle,* the seventh book in the *Chronicles of Narnia,* C. S. Lewis tells of how Aslan, the lion Christ-figure, led his people to a glorious new paradise. He concludes the story by telling of the children's last encounter with Aslan.

> And as He spoke He no longer looked to them like a lion; but the things that began to happen after that were so great and beautiful that I cannot write them. And for us this is the end of all the stories, and we can most truly say that they all lived happily ever after. But for them it was only the beginning of the real story. All their life in this world and all their adventures in Narnia had only been the cover and the title page: now at last they were beginning Chapter One of the Great Story, which no one on earth has read: which goes on forever: in which every chapter is better than the one before.[2]

One day, Jesus is coming again. He will establish His kingdom and take His throne in His Temple. And so will begin chapter one of the great story, the story of eternity.

Endnotes

1. "Book on Armageddon," *The Oregonian,* 15 February 1991.
2. C. S. Lewis, *The Last Battle* (New York: Collier Books, 1970), 184.

Appendix A

God's Plan for the Ages

Ezekiel's prophecies regarding Israel's future Temple were given in a context of biblical revelation about God's plan for the ages. Yet many Christians do not have a grasp of this overall context. As a result, they suffer from what Richard Foster calls "biblical myopia."[1] They know a lot of Bible facts but lack a worldview—a vision of the whole. Many believers have never been presented with a picture of God's all-encompassing plan for the ages. As a result, they have difficulty seeing how a future Temple for Israel fits into God's program.

In this appendix, we will present the big picture—God's plan for the ages as revealed in Genesis through Revelation. We will not pause at every milepost along the way, but we will call attention to important junctions and points of interest.

Our major theological focus in this study is the sovereignty of God—a most practical doctrine. This is a truth that gives us God's perspective when we encounter some of the inevitable difficulties of life. When a child is sick, when a loved one dies, when a job is terminated, we are able to remain confident, being assured that God knows and is sovereign over our futures.

The Eternal Kingdom of God

Scripture reveals that God possesses absolute authority and rules as king. The psalmist's proclaims, "The Lord is King forever and ever" (Ps. 10:16). Jeremiah declares, "But the LORD is the true God; He is the living God and the everlasting King" (Jer. 10:10). David announces in Psalm 103:19, "The LORD has established His throne in the heavens; and His sovereignty rules over all." As king, God has authority (a throne), a realm (the heavens), and subjects (all).

The Bible teaches that God's kingdom is timeless. As the Creator, God has always possessed absolute sovereignty. His kingdom is also universal.

God's sovereignty is unlimited in scope. He exercises His rule over all His creation.

God's rule on earth is often delegated to authorities who are raised up to officiate over His dominion. As Nebuchadnezzar had to learn, "the Most High is ruler over the realm of mankind, and bestows it on whom He wishes, and sets over it the lowliest of men" (Dan. 4:17).

The False Kingdom of Satan

Sometime in antiquity, God's universal and eternal kingdom was challenged by an angel—a created being known as Satan or the Devil. Scripture reveals very little about Satan's fall, but his sin constituted an act of rebellion against the sovereign authority of God (cf. 1 Tim. 3:6; Rev. 12:4).

At his fall, Satan instituted a counterfeit kingdom to parallel God's kingdom and challenge His authority. Satan is a usurper, claiming kingship and seeking the exercise of his authority over an earthly kingdom. Paul refers to him as the god of this world (2 Cor. 4:4) and the prince of the power of the air (Eph. 2:2). During this present age, Satan exercises a limited power over God's sin-alienated creation.

In order to fill his kingdom with followers, Satan persuaded the first human couple, Adam and Eve, to join him in rebelling against God. The divine command was clear. "From the tree of the knowledge of good and evil you shall not eat, for in the day that you eat from it you shall surely die" (Gen. 2:17). But Satan successfully carried out his scheme to bring about the fall of humanity.

Sin's effect on Adam and Eve was immediate and conclusive. For the first time, fellowship with God was broken and the human couple was separated from God by their sins. This constituted spiritual death. In addition, they and their posterity became subject to physical death. Paul summarizes the consequences of sin in Romans 5:12, "Therefore, just as through one man sin entered into the world, and death through sin, and so death spread to all men, because all sinned."

Because of humanity's sin, God cursed the earth so that it would bear its fruit only after much hard work (Gen. 3:17–18). Thorns and thistles would increase the work and frustrate the labors of mankind. All creation presently struggles under the curse because of Adam's sin (Rom. 8:22).

God's Plan

God created a perfect world. But now God's kingdom authority has been challenged by Satan; humanity has fallen into sin; and the world, under Satan's sway, is in open rebellion against God. In view of this situation, God inaugurated a program to bring the sin-marred creation back into the blessings of His glorious reign.

As with a fine jewel that has several facets, so God's program has several aspects—redemption, kingdom, and judgment. God has graciously determined to restore humankind, reestablish His kingdom authority, and deal justly with sin—all of which are designed to honor and glorify His name. Most of biblical history and theology can be viewed as the outworking of one of these aspects of God's divine program.

Redeem Humanity

Because of His infinite grace and sacrificial love, God chose to provide a way of deliverance from our fate of spiritual death. We call this God's redemptive program—a program to redeem fallen humanity.

Reclaim His Kingdom

A sovereign God cannot let His kingly authority be successfully challenged. To do so would suggest that the King is not really sovereign. So God set about to reclaim His kingdom and to reassert His sovereign authority on this earth, the sphere in which it was challenged.

Execute Judgment

Since God is holy, He cannot look upon sin and rebellion with indifference. He must execute judgment on Satan and his followers, thus purging the earth of the effects of sin.

God's Redemptive Work

Let us consider God's redemptive program first. Because of His infinite love and grace, God provided a way of salvation for all who would believe in Jesus Christ.

The Noahic Covenant (Gen. 8:21–22; 9:8–17)

God's promise to Noah after the world flood provides the crucial foundation for His redemptive work. God promised Noah that there would never be another universal destruction of every living thing by flood (Gen. 9:8–17). Even though wicked generations would arise after Noah's time, God would hold back the floodwaters of judgment until such a time when sin could be dealt with fully and finally—at the cross of Christ. The

Noahic covenant graciously provided the necessary time for God to implement His redemptive plan.

Redemption Illustrated

The Old Testament sacrifices (Exodus 12; Leviticus 1–7, 16) served to illustrate God's redemptive provision whereby an innocent victim dies in behalf of the guilty. We call these sacrifices "typical" because they point ahead to a great truth. They anticipate the coming of a substitute (Jesus) who would deal with sin fully and finally.

It is crucial to realize that the blood of animals could not ultimately atone for sins (Heb. 10:4). The sacrifices anticipated what Christ would finally accomplish. As Paul says, "in the forbearance of God He passed over the sins previously committed" (Rom. 3:25) until Christ's blood could satisfy God's holy wrath on sin.

God's Plan Expounded

God's provision of salvation for men and women of every age is by grace, through faith in God's promise, and based on the blood of Christ. This is stated clearly by Paul in Ephesians 2. In verse 8 Paul says, "For by *grace* you have been saved through *faith*" (emphasis added). He adds in verse 13, "brought near by the *blood* of Christ" (emphasis added).

The words *by grace* mean that salvation is a divine gift freely and undeservedly given. Paul says that this prevents boasting and means that God gets the glory, rather than people (Eph. 2:8–9).

The words *through faith* indicate that the divine gift of salvation is appropriated individually by personal faith. Faith (belief or trust) involves a complete reliance on God's provision of Christ's atonement.

The word *blood* reminds us that because God is holy, He must judge our sin. But because He is gracious, God provided a substitute to die in the place of the guilty (Lev. 17:11; Heb. 9:22). The Old Testament sacrifices were insufficient by themselves to provide atonement (Heb. 10:4). So God prepared the ultimate sacrifice—His own Son—to be the sacrificial Lamb that would take away the sins of the world (John 1:28; Acts 2:23).

Christ's Atonement Provided

Christ gave His life on the cross in order to satisfy God's holy wrath on sin (Rom. 3:25; 1 John 2:1–2). The most significant moment in redemptive history was that hour when Jesus bore the sins that the old-covenant sacrifices only covered. As He bore the sins of humankind—

past, present, and future—He became sin on our behalf (2 Cor. 5:21). In the ultimate moment of His agony, Jesus cried out, "My God, My God, why hast Thou forsaken Me?" (Matt. 27:46). It was as if the Father had turned His back on His Son as Jesus bore the sins of humankind. Then Jesus declared, *tetelestai,* it is finished (John 19:30). The provision of redemption was complete.

The New Covenant Enacted

Christ's death for sins meant the end of the old covenant and the enactment of a new covenant (Jer. 31:31–34; Ezek. 36:24–28; Heb. 8:6–13). The new covenant provides regeneration and the forgiveness of sin through faith in Christ and His sacrificial atonement for sins (1 Cor. 11:25; Heb. 7:22; 8:6–13; 10:15–22). Virtually all the blessings that we have in Christ are based on provisions of the new covenant.

God's Kingdom Work

From the time when God's sovereign rule over the universe was challenged by Satan, God has been working to reassert His sovereignty in the sphere where it was challenged. God's kingdom program involves a king who rules, a people who are ruled, and a sphere where this rule is recognized. Graeme Goldsworthy has put it clearly and concisely: "the kingdom of God involves God's people in God's place under God's rule."[2]

God's kingdom work involves the demonstration and recognition of His divine authority on this earth—the place where His rule was challenged. It is in this facet of God's plan for the ages that the prophecies of Ezekiel come into focus. The messianic Temple that he envisions will be operational during the future kingdom. In several significant passages in the Bible the concept of the kingdom of God is developed.

The Kingdom Promised (Gen. 12:1–3)

With the call of Abraham, God began to initiate some significant developments in the reestablishment of His kingdom authority on earth. These developments center on God's promise to Abraham in Genesis 12:1–3. This unconditional promise assures Abraham and his descendants of three things—a land, a nation, and a blessing.

First, Abraham's descendants are to have a land—the land of Israel. The dimensions of the land are given in several biblical texts (cf. Gen. 15:18; Josh. 1:4). The land promise is further developed in Deuteronomy 30:1–10. Second, Abraham's descendants are to become a great nation.

The national promises are developed in the Davidic covenant (2 Sam. 7:12–16). Third, Abraham's descendants are to be blessed and be a blessing to others. The blessing promises are developed in the new covenant (Jer. 31:31–33).

The Abrahamic covenant contributes in a significant way toward the outworking of God's kingdom program. It guarantees that Israel will have a permanent national existence, a perpetual title to the land of Israel, material and spiritual blessings (through Christ), and that Gentile nations will share in the blessings that God has for Israel (cf. Gal. 3:8–14).

The Kingdom Foreshadowed (2 Sam. 7:12–16)

During the kingship of David, another significant development in God's kingdom program occurs. In 2 Samuel 7:12–16 God enters into an eternal, unconditional covenant with David, guaranteeing that in David's line the theocratic kingdom would come to full realization and that one of David's descendants would reign over the kingdom forever.

In essence, God promised David that his house, throne, and kingdom would be eternal (2 Sam. 7:16). This means that David's line or dynasty will always be the royal line, that the right to rule will always belong to David's descendants, and that the right to a literal kingdom would never be taken away from David's posterity.

The Kingdom Presented (Matt. 4:17)

When the angel Gabriel announced to Mary that she would be the mother of the Messiah, he linked the birth of Jesus with God's promise to David in 2 Samuel 7:12–16 (Luke 1:31–33). Gabriel made it clear that Jesus was destined to receive the throne of David, to reign over the house of Jacob forever, and to rule a kingdom that has no end—all in fulfillment of 2 Samuel 7:12–16.

Jesus presented the prophesied kingdom to Israel when He announced, "Repent; for the kingdom of heaven is at hand!" This was an invitation to the Jews of His day to accept Him as King and enter into His kingdom.

The Kingdom Rejected (Matt. 12:22–37)

The Jews who were living at the time of the first century were anticipating the literal fulfillment of the kingdom promises that had been expounded by the prophets. Yet, they had difficulty accepting the person of Christ. Expecting a powerful military deliverer, they rejected the humble Savior.

The most significant turning point in Christ's ministry was His rejection by the Jewish religious establishment. They accused Him of casting out demons by the power of Satan (Matt. 12:22–24). Attributing the work of the Holy Spirit in Christ to Satan was the unforgivable sin. This decision of the Jewish leaders turned the people against Christ and set the nation on the course of rejecting their Messiah.

The Kingdom Culmination Delayed (Luke 19:11–27)

Since the kingdom was based on unconditional covenant promises, it could not be canceled even by unbelief. So Christ's rule over Israel's land was delayed until such a time as there would be a more responsive generation.

In Luke 19:11–27 Jesus told the parable of the ten pounds. Through the parable, He revealed that since Israel would not accept their king, the kingdom was to be postponed and the rejecting generation judged (cf. Luke 19:14, 27).

The Kingdom Realized (Rev. 20:4–6)

Revelation 11:15 indicates that the kingdom promises will be realized following the still-future events of a seven-year span of time called the Tribulation. At the Second Advent of Christ, the Jewish people will accept Jesus as their Messiah (Zech. 12:10–13:1). Then Jesus will set up His millennial government and rule the world for one thousand years (Rev. 20:4–6). This is the period when Ezekiel's prophesied Temple will be the worship center of the whole world.

The Kingdom of God in the Present Age

Some theologians, equating the church with the kingdom, deny the existence of a future kingdom for Israel. Others, denying any relationship between the church and the kingdom, believe that the kingdom is entirely future. We would like to suggest that there is scriptural evidence for both positions. The kingdom of God is both present and future.

Following a literal interpretation of Scripture, a future kingdom cannot be denied (Matt. 26:29; Luke 19:11; 22:30). Yet, there also seems to be a kingdom work going on in the present age (Col. 1:13; 4:11). While the church itself is not the kingdom, it is an important aspect of the kingdom. Perhaps we could say that the church is the most visible and significant aspect of the kingdom of God as it is developing in the present age.

After recording Jesus' announcement, "The time is fulfilled, and the kingdom of God is at hand" (Mark 1:15; cf. Matt. 4:17), Mark goes on to record a series of miracles. The miracles, reflecting characteristics of the kingdom (cf. Isa. 35:5–6), serve to validate His announcement. The miracles of Jesus demonstrate that the future has broken into the present. The kingdom order has been inaugurated. When Jesus gave sight to the blind, healed the sick, caused the lame to walk, cleansed lepers, and liberated those with demons, He was providing a picture of what God's kingdom is all about.

Because King Jesus has come, the glorious, redeeming reign of God has commenced. Because the King is yet to come, the kingdom is not in the form it will take when Christ returns.

Is there a kingdom of God in the present age? Yes! The kingdom of God involves God's people, in God's place, under God's rule. Today the people of God are believers in Christ (whether Jew or Gentile). God's place would be the body of Christ, the church. God's rule over His people is exercised through Christ and His undershepherds (church elders).

The kingdom of God has been inaugurated but is not yet culminated. It is a present, developing reality to be fully realized at the return of Christ—the King. Then the literal throne, dynasty, and kingdom (Luke 1:32–33) will be consummated. Ezekiel's Temple will be built in Jerusalem and serve as the worship center for this future kingdom age.

The Judgment Work

Having redeemed humankind and reclaimed God's kingdom, one could almost say, "mission accomplished." But not quite. Every major project requires some cleanup, and God's work is no exception.

God's work of judgment is both contemporary and future. It is presently and progressively taking place (John 3:18–19) and has a prophetic culmination.

Judgment on Satan and His Angels

Jesus spoke of the "eternal fire that has been prepared for the devil and his angels" (Matt. 25:41). The judgment on Satan commenced at the cross (John 12:31). Satan's sphere of activities will be further restricted during the Tribulation (Rev. 12:9) and the Millennium (Rev. 20:2). At the end of the Millennium, Satan will be cast into the lake of fire, where he will remain for eternity (Rev. 20:10).

Judgment on Satan's Followers

Revelation 20:11–15 reveals that after the Millennium, the unsaved dead will be raised and judged. Revelation 20:15 records, "And if anyone's name was not found written in the book of life, he was thrown into the lake of fire."

Purging of the Earth

Second Peter 3:10 reveals that this present earth—the sphere of Satan's rebellion against God—will be purged by fire in preparation for the new heaven and new earth (Rev. 21:1; Isa. 65:17–25). This purging will result in the removal of all the effects of sin and the Fall. Then the words of John in Revelation 22:3 will be fulfilled, "And there shall no longer be any curse."

The Bible begins with a curse because of sin. It concludes with the removal of the effect of sin and an end to the curse. In summary, this is God's plan for the ages—to reverse the curse.

Conclusion

Believers today are living between the first and second advents of Christ under the provisions of the new covenant. They are participating in God's kingdom but are yet awaiting its full consummation.

Understanding God's plan for the ages helps us to see where Ezekiel's Temple fits into God's overall design. There is another important benefit that comes from a study of God's plan for the ages. We find encouragement in knowing that God does have a plan. He knows the end from the beginning. All of history and human existence are under His rule and design. In the face of uncertainty and misfortune, Christians can be sure that God is in control. As He rules the affairs of the nations, so He rules the affairs of our lives—according to His sovereign will.

Endnotes

1. Richard Foster, "Getting the Big Picture," *Christianity Today,* 18 April 1986, 12–13.
2. Graeme Goldsworthy, *Gospel and Kingdom* (London: Paternoster, 1981), 47.

Appendix B

An Answer to the Skeptics:
A Case Study of Tyre

You may be wondering to yourself, *How can I be assured that the prophecies of Ezekiel are reliable? How can I be sure that the Temple will be rebuilt as this prophet has foretold?* Perhaps you are from Missouri, the show-me state. Or perhaps you just want to be careful and avoid placing confidence in prophecies that will prove untrustworthy.

A Basis for Skepticism

Let us assure you that there is nothing wrong with being careful and discerning before accepting something as true. Great disasters have resulted when people foolishly believed prophecies that have not been substantiated.

We had an example of such a thing in Oregon several years ago. John Gunter is a professing Christian and member of a church in Portland. Through a series of events and encounters, John came to believe that a disastrous earthquake would hit Portland, Oregon, on May 3, 1993. He asked for a sign that this was truly from God. The next morning, March 25, the house shook. Portland had experienced a mild quake. John believed that this was God's sign that a much greater earthquake was coming.

Convinced that he had a responsibility to warn others, John wrote a letter that was sent to churches throughout the Portland area. John predicted that our city would be hit with a "catastrophic and disastrous earthquake that will completely topple all of downtown Portland." He wrote, "I believe it will be worse than any earthquake ever recorded by scientists up to this date. There will be much bloodshed and pain." Many Christians were convinced that John was a true prophet and that they should heed his warning to flee the city before May 3.

May 3 came and went without so much as a tremor in the city of Portland. Prior to May 3, John Gunter had attracted lots of attention. He had been interviewed by the media. But when the predicted disaster failed to materialize, John's credibility plummeted. We have not heard of him since.[1]

Perhaps you are wondering if Ezekiel is any more trustworthy than John Gunther. Will his prophecies about Israel's future Temple find fulfillment? What does it matter whether Ezekiel's Temple vision comes to pass as Ezekiel presents it?

This is not a casual question. Ezekiel's credibility as a prophet is at stake.

But this is nothing new. Ezekiel's credibility has been questioned for centuries. The problem is the apparent discrepancies between Ezekiel and the law. For example, the Torah describes an altar with a ramp ascending from the south (Exod. 20:26). Ezekiel describes an altar with steps ascending from the east (Ezek. 43:13–17). In addition, the types and numbers of sacrifices prescribed in Ezekiel differ from those that are mentioned in the Pentateuch. On this basis, there was a time when Ezekiel was in danger of being excluded from the scriptural canon. The Talmud records that had it not been for Hananiah, son of Hezekiah, Ezekiel would have been withdrawn from use. What did he do? "Three hundred barrels of oil were provided for him (for lighting and food), and he sat in an upper chamber where he reconciled all discrepancies" (Talmud *Shabbath,* 13b). Hananiah went on to write an extensive commentary on Ezekiel, but only a few fragments survive.

Qualifications of a Prophet

God, in His infinite wisdom, devised a plan to deal with skepticism regarding those who were trusted with His prophetic message. This plan is revealed for us in Deuteronomy 18:15–22.

Having forbidden certain illegitimate methods of attempting to discern God's will, Moses declares the proper means by which God's word would be delivered to His people. As God had raised up judges, kings, and priests, so he would raise prophets. The word *prophet (nabi)* means "one who speaks for another" (Exod. 7:1–2). The function of a biblical prophet is to speak forth a message for God (cf. Exod. 18:19; Jer. 1:7).

But there was a problem in ancient times as there is today. How could true prophets be distinguished from the false? Deuteronomy 18:22 contains a test that serves to distinguish true prophets from false prophets.

"When a prophet speaks in the name of the LORD, if the thing does not come about or come true, that is the thing which the LORD has not spoken. The prophet has spoken it presumptuously; you shall not be afraid of him." Since false prophets were a menace to society, the Lord instructed that the false prophets, exposed by the failure of their predictions, were to die. Prophets must be judged by the accurate fulfillment of their prophecies.

Deuteronomy 18:19 indicates that it is the responsibility of all people to follow the words of a true prophet. So, if Ezekiel is a true prophet, we must follow his words exactly or give account to God. If Ezekiel is not a true prophet, then we are obligated to turn away from his teachings. The question is this: How do we know that Ezekiel is a true prophet with a message from God? Is there evidence that any of his prophecies have come to pass? The answer is yes.

Ezekiel and the City of Tyre

Ezekiel made some incredible prophecies about an ancient city called Tyre (Ezek. 26:1–14).

The City of Tyre

In ancient times, Tyre was the principle seaport of the seafaring Phoenicians. The city is located on the Mediterranean seacoast about thirty-five miles north of Israel's Mount Carmel and twenty-five miles south of her sister city, Sidon. The writings of the Greek historian Herodotus (ca. 490–430) indicate that the city was founded about 2740 B.C. Archaeological excavation at the site has revealed that Tyre was occupied predominately by the Greeks and Romans and later by the Crusaders.

Tyre was originally built on several islands that were joined together with debris. The Canaanites who inhabited the Phoenician coast lived there. These rocky islands gave their name to the city—*tyre* means "rock." It is still known today by the Arabic name *Sur* that became the designation for the entire region to the east, Syria. The island had two fine harbors, one on the north and one on the south, connected by a canal. In addition to the island fortress of Tyre, there was an early settlement on the mainland. So Tyre was a double site—partly on an island and partly on the coastline (fig. B.1).

The people of Tyre and the surrounding coastal region came to be known as Phoenicians, from the word *phoenix,* the purple dye that they

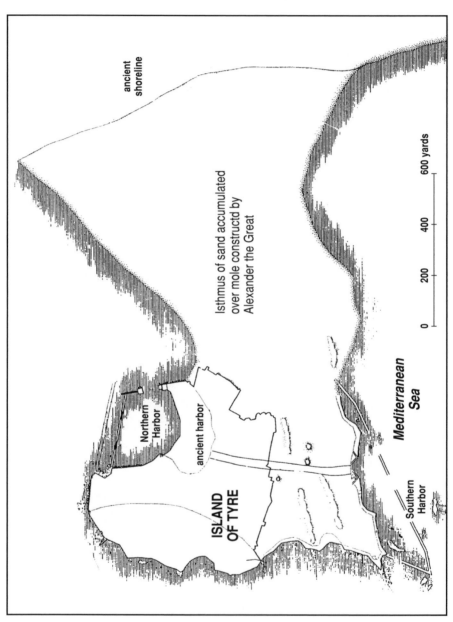

Figure B.1 Map of Tyre

produced and exported. This colorfast dye was manufactured from the *murex* shellfish, a sea snail. The Romans' love for purple fabric made the Phoenician producers wealthy and famous throughout the Mediterranean world.

The Phoenician people who came to occupy the coastal region north of Israel were not identified with a particular nation, but the major cities of the region joined together in a loosely organized coalition of city-states. These coastal cities were centers of maritime trade, as they did not have the land and resources for agriculture.

Ezekiel, in his lament over the destruction of Tyre, provides considerable detail about Tyre's export business. He mentions such wares as pine, cedar, cypress, oak, ivory, linen, silver, iron, tin, lead, bronze, slaves, and animals (Ezek. 27:5–21). Ezekiel could say, "When your wares went out from the sea, you satisfied many peoples; with the abundance of your wealth and your merchandise you enriched the kings of earth" (27:33). Isaiah refers to Tyre as being the marketplace of the nations (Isa. 23:3). Yet, for all of Tyre's economic status and influence, it was critically dependent on other nations for its basic necessities such as grain and oil (cf. 1 Kings 5:11; Acts 12:20).

Prophecies About Tyre

Although Ezekiel was a prophet in Israel, he did speak some prophecies regarding the nations that were hostile to Judah and Jerusalem. Tyre and Israel were on friendly terms during the reigns of David and Solomon, but they later drifted apart (Joel 3:4–8; Amos 1:9–10). It is in light of this later development that Ezekiel speaks a lengthy prophetic judgment against Tyre (Ezekiel 26–28). In Ezekiel 26, the prophet records five major prophecies concerning the city of Tyre.

Ezekiel predicts that because of Tyre's pleasure over Jerusalem's troubles, the Lord is going to bring up many nations against the city as the sea brings up its waves (Ezek. 26:2–3)

Nebuchadnezzar, king of Babylon, will bring his army against Tyre, besiege the city, break down the walls, and kill many of its inhabitants (Ezek. 26:7–11).

Ezekiel also states that not only will Tyre be destroyed, but the stones, timbers, and even the dust of the fallen city will be thrown into the water (Ezek. 26:12).

The area where Tyre once stood will be scraped clean down to bare rock and become a place for fishermen to spread their nets (Ezek. 26:4, 5, 14).

Tyre will never be rebuilt (Ezek. 26:14).

If Ezekiel is a true prophet, we would expect that these prophecies about Tyre would be literally fulfilled. If not, then Ezekiel must be suspected of false prophecy and we certainly would not want to trust his teachings about the future Temple. Let us consider how Ezekiel's prophecies were fulfilled.

Prophecy Fulfilled at Tyre

In 605 B.C. the Egyptians were defeated by Nebuchadnezzar at the Battle of Carchemish, and the Babylonians became the new world power. Nebuchadnezzar soon began to make his presence felt in the Middle East. He marched to Jerusalem, captured the city, and sent Daniel and some other young men of royal background to Babylon for training in the diplomatic corps. In 597 B.C. Nebuchadnezzar took King Jehoiachin and ten thousand Judeans into captivity in Babylon. Ezekiel was among those taken. Finally, in 586 B.C. Nebuchadnezzar responded to the rebellion of King Zedekiah by destroying Jerusalem and burning the holy Temple.

In order to secure a seaport for his expanding empire, Nebuchadnezzar then brought his forces against the city of Tyre. Although Jerusalem had fallen after an eighteen-month siege, the city of Tyre held off the Babylonians for thirteen years. At the end of thirteen years, Nebuchadnezzar and his army broke through the walls of Tyre. This fulfilled the words that Ezekiel had spoken that Nebuchadnezzar would make a breach in the walls of Tyre and break down its towers (Ezek. 26:4). But when Nebuchadnezzar's troops entered the city and rode their horses up and down its streets, they discovered that no one was there. When the people of Tyre realized that the end was near, they had loaded themselves onto ships and moved themselves and their possessions to an island one-half mile off the coast. Nebuchadnezzar was thwarted in his efforts to continue the fight, for he had no ships to attack the island.

The people of Tyre never came back to the old city on the seacoast. Instead they established themselves on the island. This settlement then became known as Tyre. This turn of events would seem to make Ezekiel's prophecies even more difficult to be fulfilled. Now that the ancient Tyre on the seacoast was empty, why would anyone want to destroy it?

Many years later Alexander the Great was involved in his conquest of Persia in order to establish the Greek Empire. He proceeded down the eastern side of the Mediterranean Sea toward Egypt, crushing all that stood in his way. When he came to Tyre in 332 B.C., he surveyed the situation.

The island of Tyre was fortified in such a way that Alexander knew that he could not conquer it by sea. What followed became one of the great stories in ancient military history. After considering the situation, he led his soldiers to the ruins of ancient Tyre and ordered his soldiers to begin throwing the remains of the old city into the sea. The buildings were dismantled and tossed into the sea along with all material remains from the city.

What did Alexander have in mind? His plan was to build a land bridge from the mainland to the island where the new city of Tyre stood. It took all of the rubble of the ancient city, right down to bedrock, to build the causeway to the island. This made the site of Tyre like a smooth table-rock, an ideal place for fishermen to wash and mend their nets and spread them out to dry. This they have done for centuries at the site of Tyre.

After seven months of work, Alexander captured the island fortress of Tyre. Tyre was sacked and savaged. Alexander killed ten thousand of the residents and took thirty thousand captive as slaves. The fortress was left in ruins.

The city of Tyre eventually recovered from Alexander's conquest and was rebuilt in Roman times. In 40 B.C. Tyre was attacked by the Parthians, who conquered Syria, but the city could not be taken. Many Roman ruins, including a cemetery, can be seen there today.

Over the centuries, the causeway extending from ancient Tyre to the new Tyre on the island has widened because of deposits of sand and sediment from the tides and wave action. The island of Tyre no longer exists. It is the end of a peninsula that was once only a land bridge reaching from the mainland to the island. New Tyre prospers, but ancient Tyre has never been rebuilt. It remains to this day a barren and rocky desolation.

Ezekiel's prophecies regarding Tyre have been accurately fulfilled. First, the Lord did bring "many nations" (Babylon, Greeks, Parthians) against the city (Ezek. 26:2–3). Second, Nebuchadnezzar, king of Babylon, besieged the city and broke down its walls (Ezek. 26:7–11). Third, the stones, timbers, and debris of the fallen city were thrown into the sea by Alexander (Ezek. 26:12). Fourth, the area where Tyre once stood was scraped down to bare rock. It became a place for fishermen to spread their nets (Ezek. 26:4–5, 14). Fifth, ancient Tyre has never been rebuilt (Ezek. 26:14).

Assurance for Skeptics

How is this history relevant to our study of Messiah's Temple? The literal fulfillment of Ezekiel's prophecies about Tyre demonstrate that he is a true prophet and should be taken seriously. Since Ezekiel's prophecies about Tyre have been fulfilled with such accuracy and precision, is there any reason that we should not expect his prophecies about the Temple to be fulfilled just as literally?

Deuteronomy 18 states that the test of a prophet is seen in whether or not his words come to pass in the precise manner in which they were given. Ezekiel has passed the test. His prophecies about Tyre could not have been fulfilled more precisely. What can we then conclude regarding his words about the future Temple?

Ezekiel is a proven prophet of God; we can be assured that he spoke and wrote God's truth. There is every reason to be skeptical about those who claim to possess the gift of prophecy. Many of those supposed prophecies are only the figments of their imaginations. But it is quite different with Ezekiel. His prophecies about the city of Tyre were fulfilled to the exact detail. This historical record provides us with a solid basis for our confidence that Ezekiel's prophecies about the Temple will be fulfilled with precision in every detail.

Endnotes

1. Based on a letter sent to churches in the Portland area by Cornerstone Church, Portland, Oregon (April 5, 1993).

Appendix C

Answers to Your Questions

Teaching on prophecy raises many questions. Some questions can be answered from clear statements in Scripture. With other questions, there appears to be no biblical answer. For these we can only suggest a solution based on inferences made from our general understanding. In some cases we must appeal to that great scriptural principle of confessed ignorance, "They ask me of things that I do not know" (Ps. 35:11b).

In this appendix, we wish to present the answers to some of the most frequently asked questions regarding Messiah's Temple.

Q. John, how did you first become interested in Messiah's Temple?

A. It is amazing how small things in our past can have significant implications for the future. My memory takes me back to the early 1960s. One Sunday morning during my junior year in high school, my Sunday school teacher spoke to the class about using our talents for God. I still remember his remark, "God can use whatever ability you have, if you are willing to yield it to Him."

Then he gave us a homework assignment. We were asked to go home and sit down with a piece of paper. On one side we were to write down everything we thought we could do well—no matter what it might be. Then, next to each item, we were instructed to identify some way in which we might be able to use that ability to serve God.

Following his instructions, I went home and made a list of things that I thought I could do well. It was not a very long inventory, but it was a start. As I reviewed my list, I thought of ministries to coincide with almost every talent on my list. But one left me puzzled. I was good at building models (cars, to be exact), but I could not think of any way that I could serve God by building models.

A year passed. I was now a senior in high school. One day when I arrived home from school, my mom said that our *Moody* magazine had arrived and that there was an article that could give me an idea on how I might use my model-building talent for the Lord. The article was about a man who had built a model of Herod's Temple. I will never forget the beautiful picture of his Temple model. It may seem like a small thing, but God used that moment in a significant way. On that day a seed was planted. "Someday, I will use my model-building talent to build a model of God's Temple," I said.

Over the next few years I used my model-building skill to construct architectural models for the construction of several churches. I also built a model of a proposed youth camp and some models of missionary scenes for use in Bible schools. It was exciting to be putting my model-building talent to work. What my Sunday school teacher had said was true, "Whatever your talent, God can use it for His service and glory."

After finishing college, I sensed God's leading to prepare for the ministry. My father, a pastor, was pleased when I enrolled in Western Seminary. One of the first classes I took was a survey of the Old Testament. We started with Genesis and began working our way through the books of the Bible. I was particularly intrigued by the prophets. They had so much to say about the future. One spring day my professor Dr. Stanley Ellisen began to lecture on Ezekiel 40.

"Students," he said, "we now come to a discussion of the millennial Temple that was prophesied by Ezekiel. Now here is an interesting piece of information. Every previous Temple in Israel's history has had a model built of it. I can show you a model of Solomon's Temple and a model of Herod's Temple. No one has ever built a model of Ezekiel's Temple. Someday I would like to see a model of this one as well."

You could have pushed me over with a feather! My notes are blank for the rest of the class. My mind was filled with fantastic thoughts about a Temple, a model, an ability that a high school Sunday school teacher and my mom had said I could use for the Lord.

After the lecture ended, I hurried up to speak with Dr. Ellisen. But by the time I got there, several students had already gathered around to ask him questions. It was approaching lunchtime and I had a job in the school cafeteria that I needed to get to. My questions would have to wait.

Later that day I went to Dr. Ellisen's office and told him how I wanted to use my model-building ability for the Lord. I explained how I would like to build a model of Ezekiel's Temple. After I explained my dream, he said, "John, do you think it can be done?"

That day marked the beginning of three and one-half years of research, planning, and work on a model of the Temple that Ezekiel had envisioned. The building of the model itself entailed an estimated fifteen hundred hours of work.

I completed my first model of Ezekiel's Temple in 1972. I built the model on a grand scale and set it up on two four-by-eight sheets of plywood in the attic of Western Seminary's administrative building. It did not take long before students and professors were dropping by to see what John Schmitt was up to in the attic of Amstrong Hall.

Since the completion of my first model in 1972, I have made a number of changes and alterations. I suppose there will always be the possibility of improving the model until Jesus comes and we see the real thing. However, after talking to numerous scholars, as well as those who are working on the Temple project in Israel, I am confident of this: If not precisely accurate at every detail, my model of Ezekiel's Temple is very, very close to the real thing.

Q. How do you answer the objection that Ezekiel at times seems to contradict other prophecies and portions of Scripture?

A. This question comes up most often when we speak with serious Bible students about prophecy. Ezekiel is very specific in his descriptions and statements about the future Temple. Sometimes it is hard to see how these facts fit with other passages of Scripture. For example, Ezekiel seems to contradict other Scriptures regarding the location of the Temple and the dimensions of the land.

We want to emphasize that Ezekiel's habit of being very specific is not a bad thing. In fact, it helps us to identify prophecies that have been literally fulfilled—like the rebirth of the nation of Israel that is presented through the prophecy of the dry bones.

What has become clear to us is this: God seems to enjoy making things seem impossible before He accomplishes them. There seems to be a point at which a person who would believe God must believe that what seems to be impossible is not impossible with God, and what seems to be a contradiction is not a contradiction with God.

Part of the problem is our tendency to view things from a natural and human perspective. God said, "For My thoughts are not your thoughts, neither are your ways My ways, . . . For as the heavens are higher than the earth, so are My ways higher than your ways, and My thoughts than your thoughts" (Isa. 55:8–9). Many of us, not unlike

Lazarus's sister Martha, have a hard time believing that nothing is impossible with God.

The problems that arise with Ezekiel's prophecies are not unique to this book. Abraham on several occasions had to believe the unbelievable in demonstration of his faith in God. He had to believe that Sarah, who had already gone through menopause, would give birth to a son. He had to believe that if he sacrificed Isaac, God would still provide him with an heir. God promised Abraham that everywhere his foot walked would be his possession, yet when Sarah died he did not own so much as a burial plot in the land.

The apparent contradictions in biblical prophecy are quite evident in our studies about the Messiah. We are told in many Scriptures that He will be powerful, rule with a rod of iron, and that no one will be able to stand before Him. Yet, we are also told that He would be meek and mild, that He would come riding on a donkey, and that people would beat Him. These contradictions were difficult for early interpreters. But now that these prophecies have been realized, it is clear that there is no contradiction in the Scripture. Jesus, the Messiah, is to make two appearances—first as a suffering servant to be a sacrifice and then as a powerful king to judge the earth and establish His kingdom. The prophecies about Jesus the Messiah harmonize perfectly.

At the end of the book of Daniel, the prophet admits that even he could not understand all the things that he was writing. But he was told by the angel who was speaking with him, "Do not worry about it, Daniel. When the time comes to understand, it will be understood. Make sure you write it down correctly" (Dan. 12:5–10, a paraphrase).

Several principles should be kept in mind as we consider the difficulty of comparing Ezekiel to other prophecies. First, Ezekiel cannot negate all the rest of prophecy. Second, the other prophecies cannot negate Ezekiel. Third, our responsibility as students of Scripture is to understand what it says, not to figure out how it will all work out. Finally, we must accept the fact that all aspects of God-given prophecy will happen just as predicted, even if it seems contradictory from our standpoint. We do not know how it will all be fulfilled. But God is greater than all, and He enjoys doing the impossible.

Q. The prophecy of Ezekiel's Temple is understood in a variety of ways. What is your basic approach in coming to a valid interpretation?

A. If Ezekiel is a true prophet, his words have to be from God. Ezekiel's words are truth in themselves. We do not need to turn elsewhere to see if Ezekiel is telling the truth. His prophecies need not be verified by other passages. The truth of every passage in Scripture should be found within itself. What is meant in a particular passage should be understood primarily from the passage in which it appears. If other Scripture passages are to be used, they are only to verify or act as guideposts for the meaning of the passage under consideration. The words in the passage with which we are dealing are sufficient to tell us what the author was driving at. Once we have concluded what the passage itself says, we can combine it with other passages on the same subject. Then, and only then, can we arrive at our theological conclusions. We should not come with an outside idea and try to make the passage fit our preconceived ideas. We should, rather, let the passage present us its own ideas.

Q. Since, as a Christian, I believe that Jesus died and made the final payment for sin, is there really a need for a Temple and sacrifices in the future?

A. The Bible teaches clearly that Christ is the full and final sacrifice. There is no need for further sacrifices, now or in the kingdom. But there may be the need for a reminder of what Christ has done, as the Lord's Supper is to be a reminder of the Lord's death—until He comes (1 Cor. 11:26). The Lord's Supper will terminate as a memorial when Christ returns. The Temple sacrifices will serve as a vivid reminder to us and memorial of Christ's death for us during the millennial age (see chap. 9).

Q. Is it heretical to believe that a Temple and sacrifices will once again exist?

A. One must first consider, Is the Temple a true reality or a figure of something else? It seems to us that it is definitely a part of Scripture and was seen by Ezekiel. The chronology of the book indicates that the Temple will be a central feature of the messianic kingdom. Ezekiel himself believed it was a reality and the future home of Messiah. Then, it becomes not heresy to believe that a Temple and sacrifices will exist; rather, it is almost a heresy not to believe this, especially because it is a part of God's infallible world. The burden on us is to determine how it fits—not its reality.

Q. Temples in the past have been primarily for Jewish people. How will the Gentiles be related to this future Temple?

A. God gave the people of Israel some special things—the covenants, the Law, and the Temple ministry—but not for their benefit alone. It is important to recognize that God's plan for redemption and blessing always included the world (cf. Isa. 49:6). This is evident in the great promise that God gave to Abraham. He said, "I will bless those who bless you, and the one who curses you I will curse. And in you all the families of the earth shall be blessed" (Gen. 12:3). God did not choose the Jewish people as an end in themselves. His purpose in choosing the Jews was that He might use them as a channel of blessing to the entire world.

Yes, the Temple was given to Israel. But it was given to help Israel, as Isaiah points out, to fulfill their destiny as a light of the nations (Isa. 49:6). It was God's intent that His salvation would reach to the end of the earth.

While the First Temple was strictly a Jewish facility, the Second Temple contained a court of the Gentiles where non-Jewish people could worship. The millennial Temple will be accessible to all God's people, whether Jew or non-Jew. Zechariah predicts a day in the kingdom when a Gentile will grasp the garment of a Jew saying, "Let us go with you [to Jerusalem] for we have heard that God is with you" (Zech. 8:23).

It is clear, then, that God works among His people in different ways as time progresses. For example, meat was not on the menu for the meals that Eve and Adam ate. But after the flood, meat was added to the human diet (cf. Gen. 9:3). And so at the advent of the messianic kingdom there will be less of a distinction between Jews and Gentiles than existed during the Old Testament era. Gentile believers will enjoy their allotted inheritance among the tribes of Israel (Ezek. 47:22) and will share free access with the Jews into the Temple.

Q. Revelation 22 indicates that there will be no Temple in the eternal state. What happens to the Temple at the end of the millennial kingdom?

A. The emphasis in the last chapters of Revelation is the eternal state—God's people dwelling with Him forever. In this context, Revelation 21:22 states, "And I saw no Temple in it [the New Jerusalem], for the Lord God, the Almighty, and the Lamb, are its Temple."

Scripture does not reveal what is going to happen to the messianic Temple. It is possible that this Temple will be destroyed with the burning of the earth at the end of the millennium (cf. 2 Pet. 3:10). Possibly, God could save it as His eternal throne (Ezek. 43:7).

Q. How do we know that the Temple is literal?

A. This is really a question of biblical interpretation. It is recognized among scholars that Scripture should be interpreted historically and grammatically, making full use of cultural background and language resources. In addition, Scripture should be interpreted in the normal way you would read any book. This does not preclude figures of speech. It means that we look for the literal, normal meaning of words and phrases. If a nonliteral meaning was intended, it would be evident that a literal meaning does not make sense. When Jesus said, "I am the door of the sheep" (John 10:7), it would not make sense to visualize Him as a wooden structure in a sheep pen. Obviously, this is a figure of speech. When we apply recognized principles of interpretation to our study of Ezekiel's Temple, we see no reason to move from a literal to a nonliteral interpretation.

The main objection that is raised to a literal Temple is the problem of Temple sacrifices. It is objected that such sacrifices would constitute a revival of the old covenant, contradict the book of Hebrews, and discount the redemptive work of Christ. Yet, we have pointed out that the Old Testament sacrifices never had redemptive efficacy (Heb. 10:4). Their value was in pointing the way to Christ who would deal with sin once for all time. And just as the Old Testament sacrifices point toward the death of Christ, so the kingdom sacrifices point back to and commemorate His death.

If we consider Ezekiel as a whole, we note that there are many other prophecies that have been fulfilled in a literal way. The destruction of Tyre was literally fulfilled (Ezek. 26–27). The reestablishment of the nation of Israel was literally fulfilled (Ezek. 37:1–13). The measurements and detailed description of Ezekiel's Temple suggest that the Temple is literal.

Q. There are different diagrams and models of how the Temple will appear. Do you consider this model infallible—a perfect representation of the future Temple?

John:
A. I do not consider my model of Ezekiel's Temple to be infallible or

perfect. I know that there are places where certain portions of the design could be questioned. Some dimensions Ezekiel does not give—the design of the tops of the buildings and roof shapes are not given. I consider my model to be a working model. Further research and discovery of new information could lead me to update or change the model. My model has already gone through three or four revisions since I first built it.

Even though I do not consider my work to be infallible, from my talking with people, my research, and my observations, I do believe that I am very, very close. When I was in Jerusalem at the Temple Institute, Rabbi Yisrael Ariel told me that my model is "exquisite." I take this as a very high compliment coming from a man who is one of the leaders in the world on the subject of the Temple.

Q. Exactly where on the Temple Mount do you expect the next Temple to be located?

A. There is much discussion about where the Temple should be located on the Temple Mount. Three major views are held by those who are researching this topic. (1) The Temple should stand in the area just north of the Dome of the Rock. Dr. Asher Kaufman is the leading advocate for this location. (2) The Temple belongs on the exact place where the Dome of the Rock sits. This view is held by many, the leaders of whom include Dan Bahat, head of the Israel Department of Antiquities, and Leen and Kathleen Ritmeyer. (3) The third view is that the Temple belongs to the area south of the Dome of the Rock between the Dome and the el-Aksa Mosque. This view has been brought to prominence by Tuvia Sagiv, who has studied the Temple Mount thoroughly.

All three views have good scholarship behind them but are based on circumstantial evidence based on work done outside the Temple area. Nothing can really be resolved until Israel gets permission to do on-site investigation on the Temple Mount itself. Since the Temple Mount is in Arab control, the precise location of the next Temple remains a debated question.

Q. How do you deal with the modern-day concern for animal rights in relationship to Temple sacrifices?

A. According to Jewish tradition, seven miracles took place in connection with the Temple ministry. One was that no one was ever offended by the blood sacrifices. Animal-rights activists may well be upset at the thought of sheep being killed for sacrifice. However, from God's viewpoint, the animals were created for this purpose, and they glorified God by giving their lives in this way.

At the same time, we must acknowledge that death exists because of sin. And under the old covenant, continual sin required continual, sacrificial death. The fact of death—even death of an animal—reminds us of the hideous nature of sin, and we should be offended by this. Animal sacrifices during the Millennium will serve as a reminder of the hideous conditions of sin and death that prevailed before the coming of Christ.

Q. Why should the future Temple be important for Christians?

A. Many biblical passages suggest that Christians will be involved in ruling with Christ during His messianic kingdom (cf. Dan. 7:27; Luke 19:11–27; 2 Tim. 2:12). It is clear from the parable of the pounds (Luke 19:11–27) that what a person does in this present life greatly affects his or her role in the future kingdom. The messianic Temple should be vitally important to believers since it is a preview of our own future participation in the worship of Christ.

Q. How do you view this Temple in relationship to the previous Temples that Israel has built?

A. Many people try to make Ezekiel's Temple fit with Solomon's Temple. There may be similarities, but Ezekiel's Temple is vastly different. For example, the walls surrounding Ezekiel's Temple are very low, but in Solomon's Temple the walls were quite high. Most of the gates to Solomon's Temple were on the south. Ezekiel has them positioned equally around the entire area. It is obvious that Solomon's Temple and Ezekiel's Temple are different.

Ezekiel's Temple is also very different from Herod's. Herod's Temple had a special court for women worshipers—the court of the women. In Ezekiel's Temple there appears to be no distinction between males and females during times of worship.

Ezekiel's Temple is unique among the Temples mentioned in the Bible. It is unlike any of the past Temples in Israel's history.

Q: What is the significance of the tall wooden table in the Holy Place before the door leading into the Holy of Holies (Ezek. 41:22)?

A. In Ezekiel 41:22 the prophet describes a wooden table five feet high that is positioned before the entrance to the Holy of Holies. The table is located where the altar of incense was located in previous Temples. It is strange that the table is made of wood and not overlaid with gold.

Ezekiel does not disclose the significance of this table. Some have suggested that it serves as a communion table, but there does not seem to be a biblical basis for celebrating communion in the kingdom. The words of 1 Corinthians 11:26, "until He comes," may indicate that the communion observance will be terminated when Christ returns. Ezekiel 44:15–16 indicates that the priests, the sons of Zadok, will minister to the Messiah at this table. Exactly what this ministry entails is not specified.

Q. Is Christ's glorious throne (Matt. 25:31) to be identified with the throne in Ezekiel's Temple (Ezek. 43:7)?

Nothing in this passage specifically relates these two thrones to each other. However, the possibility is very strong that they are one and the same. The passage in Matthew describes the second coming of Christ at the end of the Tribulation. The establishment of His millennial government will immediately follow. And with the millennial government comes the Messiah's Temple and the establishment of His glorious throne. Chronological evidence suggests that these two thrones are the same.

Q. Who is the prince who goes through the gate and returns (Ezek. 44:1–3)?

A. There is considerable debate as to the identity of the prince who enters the Temple by the east gate and exits by the same way (Ezek. 44:1–3). But the evidence suggests that this is not a reference to the Messiah. Verse 3 states that the prince will eat his meals in the eastern gate. One would expect that the Messiah would take His meals in the most honored place, not in a gate. Ezekiel 45:7 states that a portion of the land of the set-apart area is given to the prince. Yet the Messiah is ruler over all His kingdom. He would not need a separate possession to call His own (cf. Ezek. 45:8) since He already has the Temple. Finally, chapter 46 has several references to the prince's offering sacrifices. Jesus, the Messiah, was the full and final sacrifice. He will not be offering more sacrifices in the future.

The identity of the prince remains uncertain. The prince who will be the head over Israel during the messianic age may be the resurrected King David, Zerubbabel, or some other person appointed by the Messiah. While avoiding dogmatism on this uncertain issue, we lean toward the view that the prince is none other than King David.

John W. Schmitt, builder of the Temple model, pictured with his model.

For Further Reading

Andrews, Richard J. "The Political and Religious Groups Involved with Building the Third Temple." M.A. thesis, Indiana University, 1995.

Ariel, Rabbi Yisrael. *The Odyssey of the Third Temple.* Translated and adapted by Chaim Richman. Jerusalem: G. Israel Publications and Productions Ltd. and the Temple Institute, 1994.

Ice, Thomas, and Randall Price. *Ready to Rebuild.* Eugene, Ore.: Harvest House, 1992.

Price, Randall. *In Search of Temple Treasures.* Eugene, Ore.: Harvest House, 1994.

Index

If you have a question about Messiah's Temple that has not been answered in this book, we would be happy to respond to your letter. Please write to us at the following addresses:

J. Carl Laney
Western Seminary
5511 S.E. Hawthorne Blvd.
Portland, OR 97215

John W. Schmitt
Messianic Temple Ministries
5812 N.E. Alton
Portland, OR 97213